1000
designs for the garden
and where to find them

1000
designs for the garden
and where to find them

Ian and Geraldine Rudge

Laurence King Publishing

Published in 2011 by
Laurence King Publishing Ltd
361–373 City Road
London EC1V 1JJ
e-mail: enquiries@laurenceking.com
www.laurenceking.com

A catalogue record for this book is available
from the British Library.

ISBN: 978-1-85669-703-3

Designed by Struktur Design Limited
Researcher: Fredrika Lökholm
Senior Editor: Peter Jones
Printed in China

Front cover:
Bird feeder ball, Eva Solo Take Away, Henrik Holbaek,
Claus Jensen, Eva Denmark A/S, Denmark (p.54)

Back cover:
Hammock, Wave, Erik Nyberg, Gustav Ström,
Royal Botania, Belgium (p.200)
Potting shed boundary fence, Honeycomb Fence,
Robert Frith, Superblue Design Ltd, UK (p.273)
Garden design, The Marshalls Garden That Kids
Really Want (Chelsea Flower Show), Ian Dexter
of Lime Orchard, Marshalls PLC, UK (p.305)
Lamp, Jerry, Luca Nichetto, Carlo Tinti,
Casamania, Italy (p.132)
Garden gnome, Baddy, JoeVelluto, Plust
Collection, Italy (p.320)
Multi-purpose lamp, Uto, Lagranja Design for
Companies and Friends, Foscarini, Italy (p.133)
Portable wood-fired hot tub, Dutchtub, Floris
Schoonderbeek, Dutchtub, the Netherlands (p.114)
Lounge chair, Leaf, Lievore Altherr Molina,
Arper, Italy (p.205)
Outdoor waterbed, Lylo, Danny Venlet,
Viteo Outdoors, Austria (p.192)
Table, Cementum Foretable 140, Wolfgang Pichler,
Viteo Outdoors, Austria (p.351)

Contents

Introduction

The way we view the garden, roof terrace, balcony, or however else you define your outside space, has changed dramatically in the last 20 years, both in aesthetic content and use. This book is about our changing attitudes to the exterior and how we use and furnish these spaces. Climate change, certainly in the northern hemisphere, means conditions are milder and we are able, not only to spend more time out of doors, but also to successfully grow the sort of plants we once only saw on Mediterranean holidays. Landscape designer Andy Sturgeon agrees that the availability of plants has changed tremendously in recent years and has dramatically changed the appearance of our outside spaces. "When I started doing this kind of work in the 80s," he says, "it was all shrubs and spiraea, now the choice of plants is colossal."

And it seems that we are all developing green fingers – we all want to grow our own produce these days even if it's only a pot of herbs on the window sill. It is in cities where this is most noticeable, where the direct action of environmentalists such as guerilla gardeners is making a real difference to the greening of our cityscapes. These are groups of green activists who at night plant by stealth any overlooked, neglected public spaces. In our cities not even the vast, vertical walls of buildings have been overlooked in the quest for greener spaces. French botanist Patrick Blanc is the inventor of vertical gardening, a soilless system that cloaks arid concrete or brick façades with organic flora and fauna. "They are the only large areas left," he says, "and these areas can be used as they've never been used before." Blanc does not see vertical gardening as 'a passing fashion'; he believes it will be even more important in the future. Vertical gardens purify the air and provide vital habitats for insects and natural insulation.

Such is the upsurge of interest in outside space that it has resulted in an unprecedented growth in products for outdoor settings, providing environments that are a sympathetic extension of our interior taste. And while traditional materials and designs still have a place, there is a world of difference between classic garden design features such as rustic benches and Grecian nymphs and the type of contemporary design products featured in this book. Today we realize the potential of these exterior domestic spaces as extra rooms, a concept spawned by the design boom of the early 90s. They are furnished with sofas, artwork, occasional tables and even standard lamps, whose forms mirror their counterparts in the interior, but whose materials are weatherproof and whose colours and forms are a bold and vibrant departure from the traditional garden palette. These outdoor rooms have fully fitted kitchens and bathing facilities and sophisticated heating and lighting systems – and according to Jason Bruges, whom we interviewed about outdoor lighting, "the use of organic LEDs, and lasers, will revolutionize the way we illuminate outside in the future".

Companies such as Extremis (Belgium) and Viteo (Austria) and the Italian companies Magis, Serralunga and Driade have led the way in designing furniture and lighting ranges specifically for outdoor spaces. Some put their design energies and expertise

(above)
The Dog House
AR Design Studio
AR Design Studio, UK
www.ardesignstudio.co.uk

(right)
Vertigo Planter
Erwin Vahlenkamp
EGO² BV,
the Netherlands
www.ego2.com

(above)
**Vertical Garden,
Rue d'Alsace**
Patrick Blanc
Vertical Garden Patrick
Blanc, France
www.verticalgarden
patrickblanc.com

(left)
**Garden Design with
Water Feature**
Paul Dracott
Agave, UK
www.agaveonline.com

(left)
The Bubble Swing
Stephen Myburgh
Myburgh Designs, UK
www.myburghdesigns.com

(right)
**Havana Outdoor
Terra**
Jozeph Forakis
Foscarini srl, Italy
www.foscarini.com

(below)
**Cementum
Firetable 140**
Wolfgang Pichler
Viteo Outdoors, Austria
www.viteo.at

(above)
**Between Magnolia
and Pine**
Baumraum
Baumraum, Germany
www.baumraum.de

(left)
Playground
Sehwan Oh,
Soo Yun Ahn
OC Design Studio,
Republic of Korea
www.sehwanoh.com

(left)
Seedhead
Ruth Moilliet
Ruth Moilliet, UK
www.ruthmoilliet.com

into catering for a new generation of outdoor partygoers and their designs are a direct reflection of our changing lifestyles. Take BeHive (2006, *see* p.261), designed by Dirk Wynants of Extremis, a capacious, circular, upholstered outdoor lounger, (large enough to accommodate a dozen or so people comfortably) with the springy bounce of a trampoline to add to the experience and a canopy to stop the elements spoiling the fun. This item, inspired by the Bedouin tents of North Africa, is designed for chilling. Viteo's Cementum collection (*see* opposite) is designed for similar gatherings, a low-lying, minimalist concrete block with matching benches that provides a relaxed way of alfresco cooking, heating and seating.

Michael Hilgers of the Berlin-based company Rephorm concentrates his design mind on a very specific and overlooked outside area, the balcony. The lack of innovative work available so preoccupied the architect-turned-product-designer that he developed a range of designs for just such small, awkward spaces. These include inventive, tiered space-saving planters, seating, lighting, barbeques and even ashtrays that all attach securely to balcony railings.

Fine art has been an integral part of garden design throughout garden history, but pioneering events such as the International Festival of Gardens at Chaumont-sur-Loire in France have had a real impact on garden design and decoration of the late-twentieth and early-twenty-first century. Each year the majority of the 25 gardens created at the festival are the result of collaborations by artists working in different disciplines. Their interventions and installations have pushed established boundaries and helped publicize and promote more conceptual approaches to planting and artwork for outdoors. Patrick Blanc is just one former exhibitor whose work the festival brought to prominence

It is not just our gardens that have changed, but our relationship with outside in general. Many of the designers we interviewed talked of the increased stress levels we experience in response to technology: mobile phones, emails, the internet etcetera. Today, for many, the constraints of space and the desire for a healthier lifestyle mean we spend more time in our outside spaces than ever before and the way we socialize is slowing down too. We're all chilling out, seeking relaxed, informal gatherings where lounging and meditative music are the order of the day. The Slow Movement which advocates, among other things, doing everything at the right speed as opposed to break-neck speed, is a growing phenomenon, and is affecting the way designers design; indeed the Slow Design Movement is a reaction to manufacturing's increasing speed to prototype faster, render faster, and so forth.

One thing that is not developing slowly is outside design. This rich, diverse field is still in its infancy but the stimulus created by the cross-fertilization of interior and exterior designers means it is ripe with possibilities for the future.

Boundaries
and surfaces

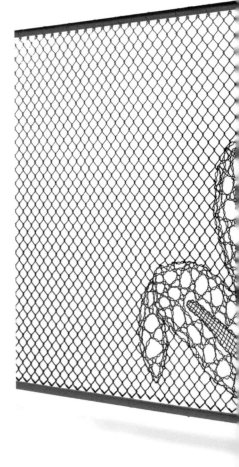

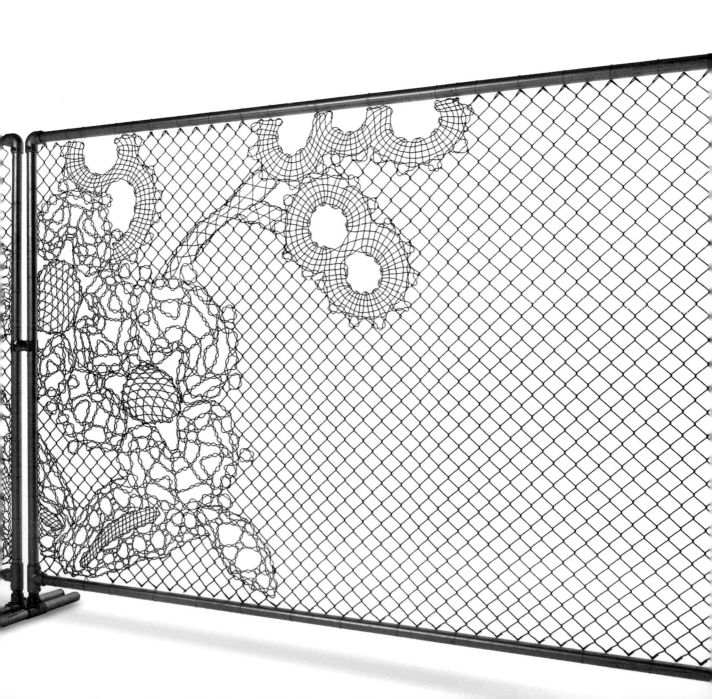

(above)
**Sculptural fence
(for Sure Start
centre, Frome),
Shilly Shally Fence**
Walter Jack Studio
Painted stainless steel
H: 90cm (35in)
L: 50m (164ft)
Walter Jack Studio with
JT Engineering, UK
www.walterjack.co.uk

(left)
**Landscape edging,
Garden Fence**
Robert Bet Figueras,
Miguel Milá
Stainless steel
H: 37cm (14⅝in)
W (one unit):
65cm (25in)
Santa & Cole, Spain
www.santacole.com

(left)
**Screening fence,
Talia80**
Architects Munkenbeck
and Marshall
Mild steel panels,
hot-dip galvanized
and polyester
powder coated
H: 120cm (47in)
W (one panel):
164.2cm (65in)
Orsogril UK, UK
www.orsogril.co.uk

(right)
**Garden fencing,
Garden Stream**
Adam Booth
Hot-forged mild steel
H: 60cm (23in)
L: 40m (131ft)
Pipers Forge, UK
www.pipersforge.com

(above)
**Fence and gate,
Gabion Basket Wall
and Sliding Custom
Steel Gate**
Andrea Bell,
Senior Associate,
Pete Bossley Architects
Gate: galvanized steel
Fence: galvanized steel
gabion baskets filled
with river rocks
H (gate):
200cm (78in)
W (gate):
618.5cm (244in)
H (fence):
200cm (78in)
W (fence):
12m (39ft)
Pete Bossley Architects,
New Zealand
www.bossleyarchitects.co.nz

(facing page)
**Fence, HardiFence®
EasyLock® System**
James Hardie Australia
Fibre cement
H: 180 or 240cm
(70 or 94in)
W: 110.5cm (43in)
James Hardie
Australia, Australia
www.jameshardie.com.au

(above)
Fence, Valla Sagrera
Josep Muxart
Cast stone
(acid-etched and
waterproofed)
H: 245cm (96in)
W: 98cm (38in)
Escofet, Spain
www.escofet.com

(right)
**Entrance,
Transforming
Entranceway**
Walter Jack Studio
Stainless steel
H: 400cm (157in)
W: 300cm (118in)
Walter Jack Studio with
Springboard Design, UK
www.walterjack.co.uk

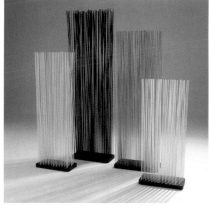

(above)
Space divider, Sticks
Hsu-Li Teo,
Stefan Kaiser
Wood, rubber,
fibreglass
H: 120, 150, 180
or 210cm (47,
59, 70 or 82in)
W: 30 or 25cm
(11¾ or 9⅞in)
L: 60 or 50cm
(23 or 19in)
Extremis, Belgium
www.extremis.be

(above)
**Folding screen,
Tikibaq Outdoor**
Frank Lefebvre,
Bastien Taillard
Lacquered stainless
steel, driftwood
H: 180cm (70in)
L: 212cm (83in)
D: 90cm (35in)
Bleu Nature, France
www.bleunature.com

(right)
**Folding screen,
Natsiq Outdoor**
Frank Lefebvre,
Bastien Taillard
Lacquered
stainless steel,
old wooden planks
H: 160cm (63in)
L: 170cm (66in)
D: 27cm (10⅝in)
Bleu Nature, France
www.bleunature.com

(left)
Screen, Zin-cane
Mark Mortimer
Bamboo, timber,
Zincalume® steel
H: 180cm (70in)
W: 150cm (59in)
D: 6.5cm (2⅝in)
Bambusero,
New Zealand
www.bambusero.co.nz

(above)
**Bamboo fence,
Kenninji**
Mark Mortimer/
Bambusero
Bamboo, timber
H: 190cm (74in)
L: 400cm (157in)
Bambusero,
New Zealand
www.bambusero.co.nz

(left)
**Fencing, Quercus
Fencing Oak Panels**
Adam Poynton
FSC Oak
H: 183cm (72in)
W: 183cm (72in)
Quercus UK Ltd, UK
www.quercusfencing.co.uk

(left)
Bespoke Trellis
Miranda Beaufort,
Jane Nicholas
Softwood with
painted finish
The Garden Builders, UK
www.gardenbuilders.co.uk

(above)
**Panel, Slatted
Blind Element**
Hillhout Bergenco BV
Spruce with Komo
preservation
treatment, planks
H: 90cm (35in)
W: 180cm (70in)
Hillhout Bergenco BV,
the Netherlands
www.hillhout.com

(below)
Panel, Ideal Panel
Hillhout Bergenco BV
Spruce with Komo
preservation
treatment, slats
H: 180cm (70in)
W: 180cm (70in)
Hillhout Bergenco BV,
the Netherlands
www.hillhout.com

(right)
**Panel, Perfo
Panel Excellent**
Hillhout Bergenco BV
Spruce with Komo
preservation
treatment, aluminium
H: 180cm (70in)
W: 90cm (35in)
Hillhout Bergenco BV,
the Netherlands
www.hillhout.com

(right)
Fencing, Horizontal Cedar Cladding
The Garden Builders
Planed cedar
H: 160cm (63in)
The Garden Builders, UK
www.gardenbuilders.co.uk

(left)
Panel, Shutter Panel Excellent
Hillhout Bergenco BV
Spruce with Komo
preservation
treatment, wood
H: 180cm (70in)
W: 90cm (35in)
Hillhout Bergenco BV,
the Netherlands
www.hillhout.com

(left)
Architectural metalwork, Garden Wall
Laidman Fabrication
Stainless steel, Ipê
H: 244cm (96in)
Laidman Fabrication, US
www.laidman.com

(above)
Panel, Louvre Panel Excellent
Hillhout Bergenco BV
Spruce with Komo
preservation
treatment, aluminium
H: 180cm (70in)
W: 90cm (35in)
Hillhout Bergenco BV,
the Netherlands
www.hillhout.com

(right)
**Room divider/Plant
pot/Light box,
Viteo Garden Wall**
Gordon Tait
Plastic
H: 55cm (21in)
W: 20 cm (7⅞in)
L: 60 cm (23in)
Viteo Outdoors, Austria
www.viteo.at

(above)
**System of cylindrical
vases, Treille**
Ronan and Erwan
Bouroullec
Stainless steel, nylon,
cast terracotta
H: 220cm (86in)
W: 70cm (27in)
Teracrea srl, Italy
www.teracrea.com

(facing page)
**Modular partition,
Separator**
Fabio Bortolani
High-pressure
laminates
H: 165cm (65in)
W: 80cm (31in)
D: 38cm (15in)
Teracrea srl, Italy
www.teracrea.com

(left)
**Vertical garden
partition,
Coco High Rise**
Rush Pleansuk
(Gaspard)
Steel EDP, anti-rust
finishing with outdoor
powder coating
H: 157cm (62in)
Diam: 36cm
(14⅛in)
Plato, Thailand
www.platoform.com

(right)
**Modular concrete curtain,
Concrete Curtain**
Memux and
Christine Pils
Concrete,
stainless steel
H (max): 420cm
(165in)
D: 2.5–3.5cm
(1–1⅜in)
Oberhauser &
Schedler, Austria
www.oberhauser-
schedler.at

(above and right)
**Modular shelving
system, Garden
Collection Shelf**
INGFAH Patio &
Outdoor Furniture
Cast-aluminium alloy
H: 30cm (11¾in)
W: 98.5cm (39in)
D: 30cm (11¾in)
INGFAH Patio &
Outdoor Furniture,
Thailand
www.ingfah.com

(above)
Wall, Green
Jean-Marie Massaud
Hand-woven Dedon
fibre, powder-coated
aluminium
H: 123cm (48in)
L: 216cm (85in)
D: 33cm (13in)
Dedon, Germany
www.dedon.de

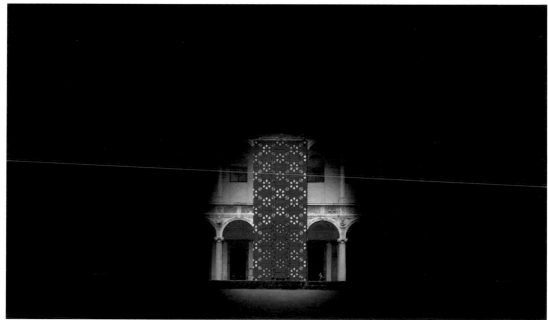

(left)
**Entrance to hospital,
Blue Sky Fence**
Walter Jack Studio
Powder-coated
aluminium,
stainless steel
H: 2m (6½ft)
L: 25m (82ft)
Walter Jack Studio, UK
www.walterjack.co.uk

(above)
**Architectural
shell (formed by
hexagonal tiles), Lace**
Antonio Citterio,
Patricia Viel
Tiles covered with a
special matt eco resin,
steel sections
H (tile): 130cm (51in)
L (tile): 150cm (59in)
Kerakoll Design, Italy
www.kerakoll.com

(above)
**Freestanding screen/
space divider, Maple
Leaf Shadowscreen
(3 part folding)**
Pattern: Jacqueline
Poncelet
Product design:
Paul Kerlaff
Powder-coated
aluminium
H: 195cm (76in)
W (folded):
65cm (25in)
W (opened):
195cm (76in)
D (folded): 5cm (2in)
Paul Kerlaff, UK
www.paulkerlaff.com

(above)
Wall, KUBRIC ®
Stefan Declerck
Metal, natural stones
H: 200cm (78in)
L (max, one piece):
580cm (228in)
KUBRIC ®, Belgium
www.kubric.eu

(above)
**Steel fabric barrier
(room divider,
balcony etc),
Lace Fence**
Jeroen Verhoeven,
Judith de Graauw,
Joep Verhoeven
PVC-coated wire
Custom-made
Lace Fence, the
Netherlands
www.lacefence.com
www.demakersvan.com

(above)
**Decorative element,
Maria**
Luca Nichetto
Polypropylene
H: 22.5cm (9in)
W: 17cm (6¾in)
D: 2.6cm (1in)
Casamania, Italy
www.casamania.it

(right)
Modular walling system with bench, Murllum
Jose Antonio Martínez Lapeña, Elías Torres
Reinforced cast stone (soft acid-treated and waterproofed)
H: 192cm (76in)
W (one unit): 294cm (116in)
Escofet, Spain
www.escofet.com

(above)
Rainwater tank and fence, Waterwall Freestanding 1200L
Gail Davidson, Mitch O'Sullivan
High-density polyethylene
H: 180cm (70in)
W: 36.5cm (14⅜in)
L: 240cm (94in)
Waterwall International, Australia
www.waterwalltanks.com

(left)
Bookshelf/Room divider, Opus Incertum
Sean Yoo
Expanded polypropylene
H: 100cm (39in)
W: 100cm (39in)
D: 35cm (13¾in)
Casamania, Italy
www.casamania.it

(left)
**Garden wall,
Stacked Log Wall**
Antony Cox,
Chris Gutteridge,
Jon Owens
Felled trees
(mixed species)
H (approx.):
180cm (70in)
W (approx.):
50cm (19in)
L (approx.):
400cm (157in)
Second Nature
Gardens, UK
www.secondnature
gardens.co.uk

(right)
**Modular walling
system, Rampante**
Oscar Tusquets
Reinforced cast stone
(acid-etched and
waterproofed)
H: 176cm (69in)
W (one unit):
195cm (76in)
Escofet, Spain
www.escofet.com

(left)
Etched glass
Etch design:
David Pearl
Landscape architect:
Ian Gray and Associates
Sand-blasted glass
D: 1.5cm (⅝in)
David Pearl, UK
www.david-pearl.com

(above)
Glass panels
Andy Sturgeon
Landscape &
Garden Design
Glass
The Garden Builders, UK
www.gardenbuilders.co.uk

(right)
**Glass fence,
Glass Fence with
Mergelock Systems**
Glass Fence
Glass, highest-grade
polished stainless steel
Various dimensions
Glass Fence, Australia
www.glassfence.com

(left)
Toughened glass balustrade
Declan Buckley,
Buckley Design
Associates
Toughened glass,
stainless steel
The Garden Builders, UK
www.gardenbuilders.co.uk

(above)
Etched glass fencing
Etch design:
David Pearl
Landscape Architect:
Ian Gray and Associates
Sand-blasted glass
D: 1.5cm (⅝in)
David Pearl, UK
www.david-pearl.com

(above)
Outdoor wall design,
Outdoor Wallpaper
Susan Bradley
Stainless steel
H: 400cm (157in)
W: 200cm (78in)
D: 1.5cm (⅝in)
Susan Bradley
Design, UK
www.susanbradley.co.uk

(above)
Trellis, Grow No. 9
Eva Schildt
Zinc-plated sheet
metal, powder-coated
anthracite
H: 50cm (19in)
W: 50cm (19in)
D: 6cm (2⅜in)
Flora Wilh. Förster
GmbH & Co. KG,
Germany
www.flora-online.de

(right)
Outdoor wall design,
Outdoor Wallpaper
Damask
Susan Bradley
Stainless steel
H: 100cm (39in)
W: 57cm (22in)
D: 1.5cm (⅝in)
Susan Bradley
Design, UK
www.susanbradley.co.uk

(above)
**Art trellis, Grow
No. 55**
Stefan Diez
Powder-coated
aluminium
H: 50cm (19in)
W: 50cm (19in)
D: 6cm (2⅜in)
Flora Wilh. Förster
GmbH & Co. KG,
Germany
www.flora-online.de

(below)
**Living wall/Vertical
garden, Live
Within Skin**
Freya Bardell,
Brian Howe
Water jet-cut stainless
steel, growing medium,
plants, irrigation system
H: 91cm (36in)
L: 213cm (84in)
D: 15cm (6in)
Greenmeme, US
www.greenmeme.com

(above)
**Pergola arch,
Nordfjell Collection**
Ulf Nordfjell
Galvanized steel
H: 250 or 200cm
(98 or 110in)
W: 200 or 240cm
(78 or 94in)
Nola, Sweden
www.nola.se

(above)
**Art trellis, Grow
No. 37**
Michael Koenig
Powder-coated
aluminium
H: 50cm (19in)
W: 50cm (19in)
D: 6cm (2⅜in)
Flora Wilh. Förster
GmbH & Co. KG,
Germany
www.flora-online.de

(left)
Wall system, Wing
Michael Koenig
Powder-coated
aluminium
H: 160, 205 or 250cm
(63, 80 or 98in)
W: 125cm (49in)
D: 63cm (24in)
Flora Wilh. Förster
GmbH & Co. KG,
Germany
www.flora-online.de

(above)
Solar energy
generating device,
Solar Ivy
Samuel Cochran,
Benjamin Howes
Leaves: 100%
recyclable
polyethylene,
solar cells:
photovoltaic modules
encased in Tefzel®
in ETFE (ethylene
tetrafluoroethylene)
Structure: stainless
steel mesh
Variable dimensions
SMIT, US
www.s-m-i-t.com

(right)
Stairs, All
Terrain Staircase
Hewitt Mfg
Aluminium
W: 91cm (36in)
Hewitt Lifts and
Roll-A-Dock, US
www.hewitt-roll-
a-dock.com

(right)
**Curtain wall,
Dolomites House**
JM Architecture
Silicon
Custom-designed
JM Architecture
with Coges, Italy
www.jma.it

(below)
**Outdoor fabric art,
Pitchfork**
Deborah Sommers
Recyclable polyester
H: 220cm (86in)
W: 60cm (23in)
d.garden collection,
France
www.
dgardencollection.com

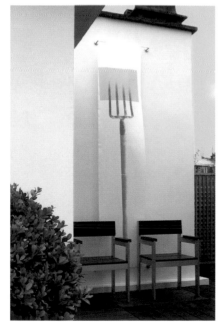

(left)
**White paint,
Allegria House**
Meri Makipentti
StoVentec T system
onto timber frame
finished with white
StoLotusan water-
repellent render
Sto AG, Germany
www.sto.com

(facing page)
**Vertical garden,
Rue d'Alsace**
Patrick Blanc
Plants, metal
frame, PVC, felt
Vertical Garden
Patrick Blanc, France
www.verticalgarden
patrickblanc.com

Patrick Blanc

If a young French boy had not been fascinated by how to purify the water in his aquarium, the 'vertical garden' or *mur végétal*, to give its French title, would never have become a feature of the urban landscape. As a youth, Patrick Blanc had no idea the research he was conducting would become the vehicle to grow plants vertically. Today Blanc is a respected botanist; he works at the French National Centre for Scientific Research where he specializes in plants from sub-tropical forests.

Vertical gardening, the device Blanc developed, is a soil-free hydroponic cultivation system, which can sustain a huge range of botanical species. It consists of a metal frame, PVC and nonbiodegradable felt, which is capable, when planted, of covering large areas of a building with an organic textile-like covering, which changes with the seasons and the elements. Vertical gardening has the ability to turn the mundane into the magnificent. "It's funny to think you can create a living system with a synthetic material," Blanc laughs. "What I do with vertical gardening is to create the same thin, moss covering, you find on the flat rock of a granite wall, where the plant roots are growing in a few millimetres of mosses."

For Blanc, aesthetics are secondary to the benefits of vertical gardening. He does not describe himself as a landscape architect, though he produces works of great artistry, but as a botanist, and his study of flora is an academic one. He has travelled the word researching and recording plants from sub-tropical forests, from Australia to South America. In some ways the vertical garden is simply a by-product of Blanc's research but it has important conservation and ecological qualities: it improves the quality of air, supports plants and provides a habitat and food for wildlife.

The concept itself has had a surprisingly long gestation period, as Blanc explains. "The first one I did was in 1988, almost 25 years ago, at the Museum of Science and Industry in Paris, but no one was interested in it at the time." It was another eight years before Blanc's innovation captured the public imagination, when he showed at the hugely influential Garden Festival at Chaumont-sur-Loire. "It was the right time and the right place," he says, "everybody was beginning to understand that the tropical rainforests were disappearing, already being destroyed and we were thinking of the problems of climate."

In Blanc's compositions botany and artistry merge: "I use many species and the vertical garden looks like the cliffs or slopes you find in nature. I've travelled to so many parts of the world and the structure of plants, of leaves, all the images I've seen in nature are mixed together in these compositions. I did research into growth habits of plants growing in the shade of the rainforest," he continues, "I know when I put plants on the vertical garden how they will be month after month and year after year, so I can mix them together. I take much care of the growth habits of the plants."

Huge numbers of plants are required for any one particular project. Take the Athenaeum Hotel in London (2009), which features a range of 260 species including aspidistra and Asian nettles. These are not planted at random, but according to their natural habitat in the wild. The advantage of vertical gardening is that a variety of habitats are created – shade, light, wind can all occur in different places at different times in these vast, living canvases.

There seems to be a huge increase of interest in gardening in general and the greening of urban spaces in particular. Blanc has his own theory about this. "Now the populations of the world are living in towns and have less and less contact with nature, but they know more and more about nature through the internet, the media, etc. So with the problem of global warming, of pollution, of algae, people are more and more interested in what nature was like in the past."

"Space in towns is used for car parks, shops and so forth," says Blanc. "The only large areas left are the vast, vertical walls of buildings, and these areas can be used – as they've never been used before. This is not just a passing fashion," he says emphatically, "it's more profound than that and it will be more so in the future."

(above)
Green roof, Wild Flower Turf
Coronet Turf/Wild Flower Turf
Wild flower meadow soil-less turf (50% wildflower seed, 50% grass seed)
Roll sizes: 1.25–40m² (13½–430½ft²)
Coronet Turf/ Wild Flower Turf, UK
www.wildflowerturf.co.uk

(above)
Green roof, Green Vegetal Roofing
Josef Hunold
Eternit fibre cement
Eternit AG, Switzerland
www.eternit.ch

(right)
Living wall, Silver Towers
ELT SEA
Opiophogon
H: 2m (6½ft)
W: 10m (33ft)
D: 7.6cm (3in)
ELT EasyGreen, Canada
www.eltlivingwalls.com

(above)
Living Wall
Andrew Marson
Plants
H: 170cm (66in)
W: 490cm (193in)
Bespoke Gardens, UK
www.bespokegardens.co.uk

(left)
Fence, HedgeLink
Pexco
Galvanized wire
with PVC needles
H: 122, 152, 183
or 244cm (48,
60, 72 or 96in)
Pexco LLC, US
www.pexco.com

(above)
**Outdoor carpet,
Fresh Lime Green**
Freek Verhoeven
Nylon/
polyurethane mix
Various dimensions
C & F Design,
the Netherlands
www.freekupyourlife.com

(above)
**Outdoor rug/
carpet, Oscar**
Susan Bradley
Rubber
W: 68cm (26in)
L: 180cm (70in)
Diam: 66cm (26in)
Susan Bradley
Design, UK
www.susanbradley.co.uk

(right)
**Outdoor carpet,
Striped Multi Colours**
Freek Verhoeven
Nylon/
polyurethane mix
Various dimensions
C & F Design,
the Netherlands
www.freekupyourlife.com

(left)
**Plastic mat,
4 x 6' Dogs**
Koko
Plastic
W: 122cm (48in)
L: 183cm (72in)
Koko, US
www.kokocompany.com
www.2Modern.com

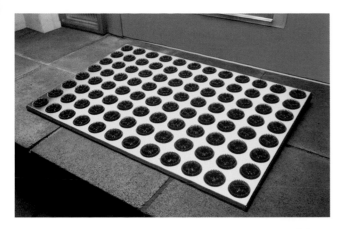

(above)
Doormat, Feet-back I
Michael Rösing
Stainless steel, plastic
H: 1.9cm (¾in)
W: 39cm (15⅜in)
L: 58.5cm (23in)
Radius Design,
Germany
www.radius-design.com

(right)
Rug (usable for outdoor and indoor), MNML 101
Eva Langhans
Polyester webbing
(100% polyester)
H: approx
1.5cm (⅝in)
W: 140cm (55in)
L: 200cm (78in)
Kymo, Germany
www.kymo.de

(above)
Rug, Artificial Grass
KC Carpet Warehouse
Plastic, with
'aqua' backing
W: 200 or 400cm
(78 or 157in)
KC Carpet
Warehouse, UK
www.kccarpets.co.uk

(right)
Plastic rug, Vera
Lina Rickardsson
PVC
W: 70cm (27in)
L: 225cm (88in)
Pappelina, Sweden
www.pappelina.com

(below and right)
**Optical illusion
outdoor living space,
Deformscape**
Thom Faulders Architect
Painted marine-grade
plywood custom tiles
W: 701cm (276in)
L: 762cm (300in)
Faulders Studio, US
www.faulders-studio.com

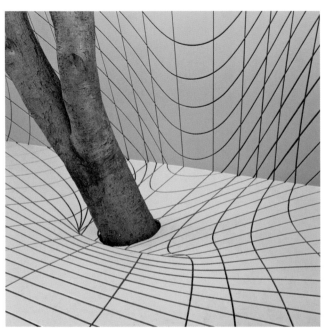

(right)
**Floor tiles,
DalLastic Outdoor
Rubber Flooring**
Dalsouple
100 per cent
recycled rubber
W: 50cm (19in)
L: 50cm (19in)
D: 3cm (1⅛in)
Dalsouple Rubber
Flooring, Germany
www.dalsouple.com

(right)
**Modular decking
system, Eco
Decking Tiles**
Eco Deck UK Ltd
Hardwood
Eco Deck UK Ltd, UK
www.ecodeckuk.com

(above)
**Feature wall,
Architectural
3D Veneer
with Horizontal
Japanese-influenced
Timber Slats**
Emily Brennan,
Sol Skurnik
Limestone
three-dimensional
veneer and spotted
gum timber
Rock 'n Stone Australia
P/L, Australia
www.rocknstone.com.au

(above)
Deck and partitions
Andrew Marson
Sawn and planed
Opepe timber
Bespoke Gardens, UK
www.bespokegardens.co.uk

(above)
Concrete paving system with surface protection CleanTop, Belpasso Premio
Hans-Josef Metten
Concrete and natural stone
W: 15cm (5⅞in)
L: 15 or 22.5cm (5⅞ or 9in)
Metten Stein+Design GmbH & Co KG, Germany
www.metten.de

(right)
Wall and setts, Rustic Brown Tumbled Walling and Setts
Ced Ltd
Dual-purpose material
Can be used as walling with a 10-cm (3⅞-in) bed and course heights of 6–8cm (2⅜–3⅛in) or as setts 10cm (3⅞in) wide and 6–8cm (2⅜–3⅛in) deep, both with lengths of 15–30cm (5⅞–11¾in)
Ced Ltd, UK
www.ced.ltd.uk

(above)
Pavers, Blue Limestone Pavers
Freya Lawson/ Heavenly Gardens
Blue limestone
H (cut to size): 3cm (1⅛in)
W (cut to size): 20cm (7⅞in)
L (cut to size): 60cm (23in)
Ced Ltd, UK
Heavenly Gardens, UK
www.ced.ltd.uk
www.heavenlygardens.co.uk

(left)
**Ceramic tiles,
Stonehenge by Marazzi**
Centro Stile Marazzi
Fine porcelain stoneware
W: 30cm (11¾in)
L: 30 cm and 60cm
(11¾in and 23in)
Marazzi, Italy
www.marazzi.it

(above)
**Sandstone paving,
Sandstone Collection**
Ced Ltd
Sandstone
W:40 or 60cm
(15¾ or 23in)
L: 40, 60 or 80cm
(15¾, 23 or 31in)
Ced Ltd, UK
www.ced.ltd.uk

(right)
**Garden featuring
Corian®, Show
Garden at RHS
Chelsea Flower
Show 2008**
Gavin Jones Garden
of Corian®
Philip Nash
DuPont™ Corian®
DuPont™ Corian®, UK
www.corian.co.uk

(right)
**Permeable resin
bound paving,
Garden Path**
SureSet
Permeable, resin-
bound paving
D: 6mm (¼in)
SureSet UK Ltd, UK
www.sureset.co.uk

(left)
**Decorative
aggregate, Traxmax**
Ced Ltd
100% recycled ceramic
Ced Ltd, UK
www.ced.ltd.uk

(right)
**Flat pebbles, Green
and White (Splash
Garden)**
Ced Ltd,
Garden design: Lucy
Summers
Beach pebbles
Ced Ltd, UK
www.ced.ltd.uk

(right)
Yellow Granite and Barleycorn Quartz
Ced Ltd,
Garden design:
Lizzie Taylor
Yellow granite setts
and barleycorn
quartz gravel
(setts) 10-cm
(3⅞-in) cubes
Ced Ltd, UK
www.ced.ltd.uk

(below)
Glass gravel, Grey, medium-sized landscaping glass
ASG Glass
Glass
ASG Glass, US
www.asgglass.com

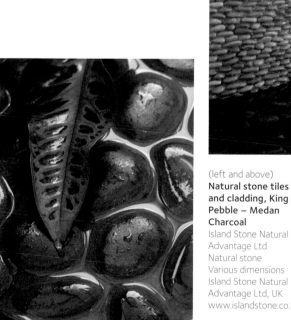

(left and above)
Natural stone tiles and cladding, King Pebble – Medan Charcoal
Island Stone Natural
Advantage Ltd
Natural stone
Various dimensions
Island Stone Natural
Advantage Ltd, UK
www.islandstone.co.uk

(above)
Natural stone tiles and cladding, Premium Pebble – Antique White
Island Stone Natural
Advantage Ltd
Natural stone
Various dimensions
Island Stone Natural
Advantage Ltd, UK
www.islandstone.co.uk

(left and below)
**Modular,
self-contained,
self-supporting
LED-illuminated deck
and walkway system,
CATWALK**
Alex Lorenz, Luciana
Misi, Nathan Munk
Steel, polyethylene
Array of power-sipping
LED points of light
CATWALK modules
available in three sizes:
Small: 60 x 60cm
(24 x 24in)
Medium: 60 x 120cm
(24 x 47in)
Large: 120 x 120cm
(47 x 47in)
MINIMIS, US
www.minim.is

(left)
**Light-transmitting
concrete**
Aron Losonczi
Litracon® (Light-
Transmitting Concrete)
W (max block size):
40cm (15¾in)
L (max block size):
120cm (47in)
D: 2.5–50cm (1–19in)
Litracon Ltd, Hungary
www.litracon.hu

(left)
Natural stone tiles and cladding, Linear Interlock Glass – Smoke
Island Stone Natural Advantage Ltd
Natural stone
Various dimensions
Island Stone Natural Advantage Ltd, UK
www.islandstone.co.uk

(left)
Panels, Hyperwave Stream
Christian Pongratz
Pietra di Venezia
H: 100cm (39in)
W: 145cm (57in)
Testi Fratelli, Italy
www.testigroup.com

(above)
Natural stone tiles and cladding, Rustic Cladding – Himarchal Black
Island Stone Natural Advantage Ltd
Natural stone
Various dimensions
Island Stone Natural Advantage Ltd, UK
www.islandstone.co.uk

(above)
**Ceramic tile,
Collection Borgo
Antico**
Mirage
Porcelain stoneware
W: 30cm (11¾in)
L: 30cm (11¾in)
Mirage, Italy
www.mirage.it

(above)
**Natural stone
tiles and cladding,
Strip Cladding –
Quartzitic Silver**
Island Stone Natural
Advantage Ltd
Natural stone
Various dimensions
Island Stone Natural
Advantage Ltd, UK
www.islandstone.co.uk

(right)
**Wall, Curving
Boundary Dry
Stone Wall**
Richard Clegg
Stones
Custom-made
Richard Clegg, UK
www.richardclegg.
co.uk

(right)
Tiles, X-stone
Ceramiche Refin SpA
Porcelain stoneware
W: 10 or 30cm
(3⅞ or 11¾in)
L: 15 or 30cm
(5⅞ or 11¾in)
Ceramiche Refin
SpA, Italy
www.refin.it

(left)
Covering, Rose
Raffaello Galiotto
Marble
W: 80cm (31in)
L: 80cm (31in)
Decormarmi srl, Italy
www.decormarmi.com

(below)
**Concrete panels,
Solid Poetry**
Frederik Molenschot
& Susanne Happle
Concrete
Various dimensions
Studio Molen,
the Netherlands
www.studiomolen.nl

The panels change
when they come into
contact with water.

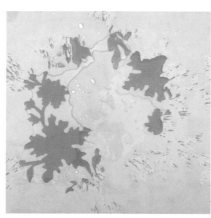

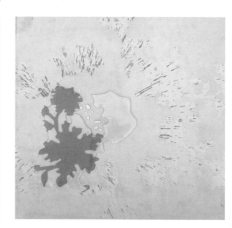

(left)
**Pattern in Bisazza
glass mosaic,
Columns Green**
Jaime Hayon.
Bisazza glass mosaic
Pattern is sold
by module
1 module = 36 sheets
= 129.1 x 290.5cm
(51in x 114in)
Bisazza SpA, Italy
www.bisazza.com

(above)
**Natural stone
tiles and cladding,
Quartzitic Silver
Slate Wave Tile**
Island Stone Natural
Advantage Ltd
Natural stone
Various dimensions
Island Stone Natural
Advantage Ltd, UK
www.islandstone.co.uk

(left)
**Pattern in Bisazza
glass mosaic,
Bamboo Black**
René Gonzalez
Bisazza glass mosaic
Pattern is sold
by module
1 module = 36 sheets
= 129.1 x 290.5cm
(51in x 114in)
Bisazza SpA, Italy
www.bisazza.com

(below)
**Pattern in Bisazza
glass mosaic,
Bouquet**
Carlo Dal Bianco
Bisazza glass mosaic
Pattern is sold
by module
1 module = 36 sheets
= 129.1 x 290.5cm
(51in x 114in)
Bisazza SpA, Italy
www.bisazza.com

(right)
**Mosaic pattern,
Zante Bianco**
Carlo Dal Bianco
Glass mosaic
W (one tile):
2cm (¾in)
L (one tile):
2cm (¾in)
Bisazza SpA, Italy
www.bisazza.com

(left)
**Mosaic, Labyrinth
White Gold**
Onix Design Group
Glass mosaic
W: 2cm (¾in)
L: 2cm (¾in)
Onix, Spain
www.onixmosaic.com

(below)
**Wall/floor tile,
Lace Embossed Tile**
Jethro Macey
Concrete
W: 30cm (11¾in)
L: 30cm (11¾in)
The Third Nature, UK
www.thethirdnature.co.uk

Wildlife resources

(above)
**Bird feeder,
Birdball Peanut
Feeder**
Gavin and Kate
Christman
Ceramic
Diam: 15.5cm
(6⅛in)
Green and Blue, UK
www.greenandblue.co.uk

(left)
**Bird feeder ball,
Eva Solo Take Away**
Henrik Holbaek, Claus
Jensen, Tools Design
Mouth-blown glass
Diam: 20cm (7⅞in)
Eva Denmark A/S,
Denmark
www.evadenmark.com

(below)
**Bird feeder,
Egg Bird Feeder**
Jim Schatz
Hand-crafted glossy
ceramic earthenware,
aluminium
H: 21.6cm (8½in)
W (base): 19cm (7½in)
W (egg): 15.2cm (6in)
J Schatz, US
www.jschatz.com

(above)
**Bird feeder, Folding
Bird House**
Jesper Moller Hansen,
Dorthe Weis
Steel
H: 18cm (7in)
W: 25cm (10in)
D: 20cm (7⅞in)
MoMA Retail, US
www.momastore.org

(left)
**Bird Feeder, Perch
Birdfeeder**
Amy Adams
Earthenware,
vegetable-tanned
leather
H: 12.7cm (5in)
Diam: 17.8cm (7in)
Perch Design Inc, US
www.perchdesign.net

(below)
Bread board,
Bird Bread
Naama Steinbock,
Idan Friedman
of Reddish studio
Wood
H: 16cm (6¼in)
W: 17cm (6¾in)
L: 47cm (18½in)
Reddish studio, Israel
www.reddishstudio.com

(above)
Bird feeder, Spuntino
Dino Salvatico
Steel, plastic foam,
metal spoon
H: 15cm (5⅞in)
D: 12cm (4¾in)
Dino Salvatico,
Switzerland
www.dinosalvatico.com

(left)
**Bird house,
Piep-show**
Ralph Krauter
Plastic, aluminium
H: 16cm (6¼in)
W: 30cm (11¾in)
D: 16cm (6¼in)
Radius Design,
Germany
www.radius-design.com

(right)
Bird house, Steckling
Michael Hilgers
Recyclable
polyethylene
Diam: 30cm
(11¾in)
Rephorm, Germany
www.rephorm.de

(left)
Bird feeder, Nido
Susanne Augenstein
Stainless steel
H: 141cm (55in)
W: 18cm (7in)
L: 12.5cm (4⅞in)
Blomus GmbH,
Germany
www.blomus.com

(right)
**Bird feeder,
Bird Table**
Jasper Morrison
Stainless steel,
injection-moulded
polypropylene
H: 98.5cm (39in)
W: 42cm (16½in)
Magis SpA, Italy
www.magisdesign.com

(left)
**Contemporary
garden bird
table, Birdie**
Schmiddern, Berlin
Brushed stainless
steel, hardwood
H: 129cm (51in)
Diam: 40cm
(15¾in)
Ingarden, UK
www.ingarden.co.uk

(left)
**Bird table/bath,
Perch**
Gavin and Kate
Christman
Fibreglass resin,
stainless steel
H: 150cm (59in)
Diam (bath):
45cm (17¾in)
Diam (table):
25cm (9⅞in)
Green and Blue, UK
www.greenandblue.co.uk

Henrik Holbaek and Claus Jensen

With more than 200 awards and distinctions, Henrik Holbaek and Claus Jensen of Tools Design are among Denmark's most fêted designers. The hidden talent behind many of the innovative designs in the Eva Solo product range, their strength lies in their ability to revisit the mundane, everyday objects we take for granted and revivify them by improving their function and injecting them with contemporary design simplicity.

The innovative duo were the first to use silicone for potholders, they have designed sleek waste bins that open on all sides, and flower pots that extend the life of houseplants. While Jensen is a graduate Industrial Designer of Denmark's Designskole, Copenhagen, Holbaek trained as an architect and a graduate Industrial Designer MDD of the Royal Danish Academy of Fine Arts. They have been working together since 1989, building a formidable portfolio that ranges from electronics and medical equipment to household products. Latterly they have developed a range of products specifically designed for exterior use. Henrik Holbaek, spokesman for the design duo explains: "We design a lot of products for the interior and now we are designing for the garden, which is rapidly becoming an extension of our homes – we treat it now as another room. It was in response to this that we started the line of products called Outdoor for Eva Solo."

Within this group of svelte grills, barbeques, coffee makers and picnic accessories is a group of bird feeders, baths and nesting boxes, which beautifully illustrate the duo's design aesthetic, turning the traditional concept of bird homes and feeders on its head – no thatched roofs or knarled wood here, not a rustic reference in sight. These are wildlife features for twenty-first-century living, and their design reflects our increasing demand for stylish garden products. "We wanted to design products that brought wildlife back to the garden, but also fitted in with modern design," says Holbaek. "Our work makes references to contemporary architecture, but our main source of inspiration when we start a new project is function; that is always the starting point, everything follows from that, function is the hidden beauty, the product's personality."

"Interest in the garden is increasing," Holbaek continues, "and if you want a birdfeeder you want one that will fit into your lifestyle, one that reflects your personal aesthetic." People want to show off in their exterior rooms with sofas and outdoor kitchens. "I know, in tropical climates this is the norm but in our traditionally cold, northern European climate this is a relatively new phenomenon. As a nation," he quips, "we Danes have spent of lot of time designing the perfect bathroom, the perfect kitchen, and now we're concentrating on the next room, which is, of course, the garden."

Designing wildlife features has its own set of demands. "For a start," Holbaek explains, "you have to please two clients, the consumer and the birds themselves. We felt that we needed to find a design that reflected modern architecture on the one hand and on the other we needed to know exactly what functions our bird products needed to address. We conducted a lot of experiments in our own garden," he continues, "asking questions such as, 'What is good for the birds? What kind of restaurant would they eat at?'"

Their research concluded that, among other criteria, the products must be easy to clean – bird feeders, nesters and baths can harbour various bacteria. Holbaek and Jensen use glass and porcelain as these materials are easy to clean (all their products are dishwasher safe); glass has the added function of transparency, which allows you to see how full feeders are.

Attention to detail is at the heart of their work, everything is considered. Take their nesting box Ornithological (*see* p.64), made of terracotta glazed white to reflect heat and to keep fledglings warm, with four different-sized holes, depending on which sized birds you wish to attract. The slippery exterior discourages predators, while the interior contains a ladder to make it easier for fledglings to climb out

Catering for the throwaway society is not part of their mission. "Our brief," says Holbaek, "is to ask ourselves how we can make people use a product longer" - their choice of certain materials is part of that process. "It's a delicate balance," he continues, "if a design is too fashionable, it will be discarded when the next fashionable item usurps it. Timeless design is the key – it is better for the planet."

(above)
Bird table, Eva Solo Self-service
Henrik Holbaek,
Claus Jensen,
Tools Design
Mouth-blown glass,
synthetic materials
H: 110cm (43in)
Diam: 22 or 32cm
(8⅝ or 12⅝in)
Eva Denmark A/S,
Denmark
www.evadenmark.com

(right)
Bird bath, Eva Solo Birdbath
Henrik Holbaek,
Claus Jensen,
Tools Design
White-glazed porcelain
Diam: 35cm (13¾in)
Eva Denmark A/S,
Denmark
www.evadenmark.com

(left)
Bird feeder, Type 01
Patrick Anderson
FSC-certified
Honduran mahogany,
purple heart, cedar,
formaldehyde-free
MDF, aluminium,
low-VOC paint
H: 26.3cm (10½in)
W: 50cm (20in)
L: 30cm (12in)
Neoshed, US
www.neoshed.com

(above)
Bird feeder, Type 02
Patrick Anderson
FSC-certified
Honduran mahogany,
purple heart, cedar,
formaldehyde-free
MDF, aluminium,
low-VOC paint
H: 26.3cm (10½in)
W: 50cm (20in)
L: 30cm (12in)
Neoshed, US
www.neoshed.com

(above)
Bird feeder, Type 04
Patrick Anderson
FSC-certified
Honduran mahogany,
purple heart, cedar,
formaldehyde-free
MDF, aluminium,
low-VOC paint
H: 26.3cm (10½in)
W: 50cm (20in)
L: 30cm (12in)
Neoshed, US
www.neoshed.com

(right)
Bird feeder, Type 03
Patrick Anderson
FSC-certified
Honduran mahogany,
purple heart, cedar,
formaldehyde-free
MDF, aluminium,
low-VOC paint
H: 26.3cm (10½in)
W: 50cm (20in)
L: 30cm (12in)
Neoshed, US
www.neoshed.com

(above)
**Bird feeder,
La Cantine aux
Moineaux**
Radi Designers
Steel
H: 180cm (70in)
W: 73cm (28in)
Radi Designers, France
www.radidesigners.com

(left)
**Bird feeder, Reclaimed
Rooftile Birdhouse**
Tomoko Azumi
Reclaimed rooftop tile, pine
H: 35cm (13¾in)
H (pole): 130cm (51in)
W: 22cm (8⅝in)
D: 25cm (9⅞in)
t.n.a. design studio, UK
www.tnadesignstudio.co.uk

(above)
**Bird feeder/
Bird bath, Fuera**
Susanne Augenstein
Stainless steel,
beechwood
H: 131cm (52in)
Diam: 25cm (9⅞in)
Blomus GmbH,
Germany
www.blomus.com

(left)
**Bird houses, The
Museum Birdhouse**
Tom Dukich
Stainless steel
H: 30.5cm (12in)
W: 23cm (9in)
D: 30.5cm (12in)
Diam: 23cm (9in)
Tom Dukich, US
www.tomdukich.com

(above)
**Bird houses, Modern Birdhouses™:
Ralph, Richard, J.R.**
Dail Dixon
Teak, aluminium
Diam (opening):
3.5cm (1⅜in)
Wieler, US
www.wieler.com

(above)
Bird house, Type 01
Patrick Anderson
FSC-certified
Honduran mahogany,
purple heart, cedar,
formaldehyde-free
MDF, aluminium,
low-VOC paint
H: 17.5cm (7in)
W: 17.5cm (7in)
L: 17.5cm (7in)
Neoshed, US
www.neoshed.com

(above)
**Bird house,
Solar Birdhouse**
Guido Ooms,
Karin van Lieshout
FSC-certified Meranti,
solar panel, electronics
H: 18cm (7⅛in)
W: 9cm (3½in)
D: 9cm (3½in)
Oooms, the
Netherlands
www.oooms.nl

(right)
**Bird house,
Bird Box**
Fredrikson Stallard
Solid European oak,
cast aluminium
H: 28cm (11in)
W: 16cm (6¼in)
D: 15cm (5⅞in)
Thorsten Van Elten, UK
www.thorstenvanelten.com

(below)
**Bird houses,
Byrdhouses**
Chris Eckersley
Powder-coated
steel, oak
H (houses):
40–55cm
(13¾–21in)
H (stand):
180cm (70in)
W: 36cm (14⅛in)
D: 36cm (14⅛in)
Chris Eckersley
Design, UK
www.chriseckersley.co.uk

(above)
**Bird house, Reclaimed
Rooftile Birdhouse**
Tomoko Azumi
Reclaimed rooftop
tile, pine
H: 21cm (8¼in)
W: 22cm (8⅝in)
D: 18cm (7⅛in)
t.n.a. design studio, UK
www.tnadesignstudio.co.uk

(left)
**Bird tree,
Bird Treehouse**
Kodjo Kouwenhoven
Steel, wood
H: 153cm (60in)
W: 60cm (23in)
D: 25cm (9⅞in)
Maandag meubels,
the Netherlands
www.maandagmeubels.nl

(left)
**Bird house,
Geo-birdhouse**
Kelly Lamb
Ceramic
Diam: 20.3cm (8in)
Areaware, US
www.areaware.com

(above)
Bird house, Birdball
Gavin and Kate
Christman
Ceramic
Diam: 18cm (7in)
Green and Blue, UK
www.greenandblue.co.uk

(facing page)
**Bird house,
Egg Bird House**
Jim Schatz
Hand-crafted glossy
ceramic earthenware,
vinyl, rubber,
aluminium, nylon
H: 20.3cm (8in)
W: 15.2cm (6in)
Diam: 15.2cm (6in)
J Schatz, US
www.jschatz.com

(left)
**Nesting box, Eva Solo
Ornithological**
Claus Jensen,
Henrik Holbaek
of Tools Design
Plastic, glazed
terracotta
H: 24cm (9½in)
W: 15cm (5⅞in)
Eva Denmark A/S,
Denmark
www.evadenmark.com

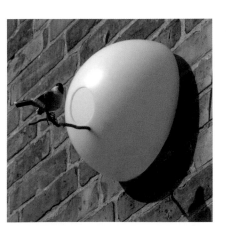

(left)
**Wall-fixed bird
house, Kokki Bird**
Michael Hilgers
Recyclable
polyethylene
Diam: 30cm
(11¾in)
Rephorm, Germany
www.rephorm.de

(below)
**Bird house,
Birdhouse**
Marcel Wanders
Polypropylene,
porcelain, sisal, steel
H: 20cm (7⅞in)
W: 30cm (11¾in)
D: 20cm (7⅞in)
Droog BV,
the Netherlands
www.droog.com

(right)
Bird house, Birdbottle
Jeffery Theesfeld
Aluminium, powder
coating, stainless steel
Diam: 10cm (4in)
L: 34cm (13½in)
Blend Design, US
www.blend-design.com

(above)
**Bird house, Holy
Homes – Church**
Frederik Roijé
Porcelain, glass
with golden finish
H: 26cm (10¼in)
W: 15cm (5⅞in)
D: 14cm (5½in)
Tuttobene, the
Netherlands
www.
tuttobenedesignshop.com

(above)
**Bird house,
Holy Homes – Mosque**
Frederik Roijé
Porcelain, glass
with golden finish
H: 26cm (10¼in)
W: 15cm (5⅞in)
D: 14cm (5½in)
Tuttobene, the
Netherlands
www.
tuttobenedesignshop.com

(right)
Bird house
Emilie Cazin
Oak
H: 28cm (11in)
W: 150cm (59in)
L: 200cm (78in)
Vlaemsch, Belgium
www.design-milk.com

(below)
Bird house,
Hepper Roost
Jed Crystal
Anodized aluminium
H: 25.4cm (10in)
W: 17.8cm (7in)
L: 33cm (13in)
Hepper, US
www.hepper.com

(above)
Bird house,
Piep-show-xxl
Ralph Kraueter
Zinc-coated and
powder-coated steel,
anodized aluminium
H: 45cm (17¾in)
W: 49cm (19¼in)
D: 55cm (21½in)
Radius Design,
Germany
www.radius-design.com

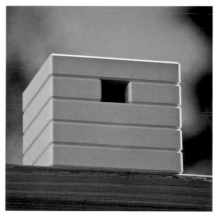

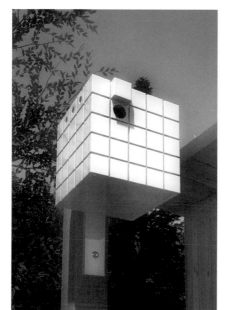

(left)
Bird house,
Cube Birdhouse
Loll Designs
100% post-consumer
recycled plastic
H: 13cm (5in)
W: 14cm (5½in)
D: 14cm (5½in)
Loll Designs, US
www.lolldesigns.com

(right)
Bird house, Type RM
Patrick Anderson
FSC-certified
Honduran mahogany,
purple heart, cedar,
formaldehyde-free
MDF, aluminium,
low-VOC paint
H: 20cm (8in)
W: 20cm (8in)
L: 20cm (8in)
Neoshed, US
www.neoshed.com

(left)
**Chicken house,
Eglu Cube**
Omlet
MDPE
H: 80cm (31in)
W: 120cm (47in)
D: 100cm (39in)
Omlet, UK
www.omlet.com

(above)
**Garden house,
Ex-Ecal**
Alexandre Gaillard,
Adrien Rovero,
Augustin Scott
de Martinville,
Antoine Vauthey,
Steel and
Bouroullec Algues
H: 285cm (112in)
W: 250cm (98in)
L: 360cm (141in)
ECAL (Ecole Cantonale
d'Art de Lausanne),
Switzerland
www.ecal.ch

(right)
Dog home, eiCrate
Peter Pracilio
Powder-coated steel
H: 62cm (24½in)
W: 91cm (36in)
D: 86cm (34in)
designGO!, US
www.gopetdesign.com

(left)
**Pet house,
Architectura
Pet House**
David M. Neighbor
Birch, cedar
H: 93cm (36in)
W: 122cm (48in)
L: 122cm (48in)
Pre-Fab-Pets, US
www.pre-fab-pets.com

(left)
**Wading pool/Play pool
for dogs, Bone Pool**
Raymond Palmer
High-molecular-weight
polyethylene,
brass, rubber
W: 112cm (44in)
L: 168cm (66in)
D: 28cm (11in)
One Dog One Bone
Enterprises inc, US
www.onedogonebone.com

(above)
**Dog house, Nomad
Dog's House**
Marco Morosini
Blazed clay glossy
white, hand-painted
with 24-ct platinum
H: 45cm (17¾in)
W: 29cm (11⅜in)
L: 52cm (20in)
Bosa Ceramiche, Italy
www.bosatrade.it

(above)
**Dog/Human house,
The Dog House**
AR Design Studio
Oak
H: 500cm (196in)
W: 200cm (787in)
L: 100cm (393in)
AR Design Studio, UK
www.ardesignstudio.co.uk

(right)
**Dog house, Green
Woof (Barkitecture)**
Michael Rausch
Plywood, timber, Ipê
decking, stainless steel,
GreenGrid® planters,
sedum plants
H: 92cm (36in)
W: 127cm (50in)
D: 127cm (50in)
Johnson Squared
Architecture +
Planning, US
www.johnsonsquared.com

(right)
**Dog house,
Green Spot Green
(Barkitecture)**
Peter Brachvogel, Stella
Carosso of
BC&J Architects
Plywood, cedar, metal,
soil matrix, grass
W: 76cm (29in)
L: 122cm (48in)
BC&J Architects, US
www.bcandj.com

(right)
Dog house, Magis Dog House
Michael Young
Rotation-moulded
polyethylene,
stainless steel
H: 75.5cm (29in)
W: 48.5cm (19¼in)
L: 89cm (35in)
Magis SpA, Italy
www.magisdesign.com

(left)
Cat shelter/bed, KatKabin DezRez
Trevor Hudson
ABS, aluminium,
high-impact
polystyrene,
polycarbonate,
cotton, foam
H: 32cm (12½in)
W: 41cm (16in)
L: 55cm (21½in)
Brinsea Products
Ltd, UK
www.katkabin.co.uk

(below)
Pet door surround, Swarovski Crystal-encrusted Cat Flap Surround
Peter McDermott
Wood, Swarovski
crystals
H: 28–31cm
(11–12¼in)
W: 22–30cm
(8⅝–11¾in)
Doors4paws, UK
www.doors4paws.co.uk

(right)
**Pet house, Eglu
for Guinea Pigs**
Omlet
MDPE
H: 70cm (27in)
W: 70cm (27in)
D: 70cm (27in)
Omlet, UK
www.omlet.com

(above)
**Pet house,
Eglu for Rabbits**
Omlet
MDPE
 H: 70cm (27in)
W: 70cm (27in)
D: 70cm (27in)
Omlet, UK
www.omlet.com

(right)
Beehive, Beehaus
Omlet
MDPE, steel
H: 90cm (35in)
W: 55cm (21in)
D: 120cm (47in)
Omlet, UK
www.omlet.com

Containers

(above)
Pot, Kabin
Luisa Bocchietto
Polyethylene
H: 100cm (39in)
W: 44cm (17⅜in)
Serralunga srl, Italy
www.serralunga.com

(left)
**Flower pot, Cono
Cuadrado Aigua**
Studio Vondom
Low-density
linear polythene
H: 30, 40, 50, 60,
80cm (11¾, 15¾,
19, 23, 31in)
W: 30, 40, 50,
60, 80cm (11¾,
15¾, 19, 23, 31in)
L: 30,40, 50, 60,
80cm (11¾, 15¾,
19, 23, 31in)
Vondom, Spain
www.vondom.com

(above)
Pot, Carl
Pierre Sindre
Iron
H: 30 or 60cm
(11¾ or 23in)
Röshults, Sweden
www.roshults.se

(left)
**Table/flower pot,
Moma High**
Javier Mariscal
Low-density, linear
polythene
H: 100cm (39in)
W: 60cm (23in)
L: 75cm (29in)
Vondom, Spain
www.vondom.com

(above)
Planter, Elevation
Arik Levy
Powder-coated
aluminium
H: 73, 81 or 102cm
(28, 31 or 40in)
W: 55, 48, 55cm
(21, 18⅞ or 21in)
Flora Wilh. Förster
GmbH & Co. KG,
Germany
www.flora-online.de

(right)
Planter, Mercato
Flora
Powder-coated
aluminium
H: 45cm (17¾in)
W: 40cm (15¾in)
D: 40cm (15¾in)
Flora Wilh. Förster
GmbH & Co. KG,
Germany
www.flora-online.de

(below)
Flower pot, Alea
Dirk Wynants
Galvanized steel,
polyester
H: 48cm (18⅞in)
W: 52cm (20in)
L: 52cm (20in)
Extremis, Belgium
www.extremis.be

(right)
**Table/flower pot,
Moma Low**
Javier Mariscal
Low-density, linear
polythene
H: 45cm (17¾in)
W: 100cm (39in)
L: 115cm (45in)
Vondom, Spain
www.vondom.com

(left)
**Pot/planter,
Vertigo Planter**
Erwin Vahlenkamp
Fibreglass-reinforced
polyester
H: 47, 62 or 77cm,
(18½, 24 or 30in),
W: 45, 60 or 75cm,
(17¾, 23 or 29in)
L: 45, 60 or 75cm
(17¾, 23 or 29in)
EGO² BV, the
Netherlands
www.ego2.com

(left)
Planter, Eden
Villiers Brothers
Bronze
H: 99cm (39in)
W: 122cm (48in)
D: 122cm (48in)
Villiers, UK
www.henryhalldesigns.com

(facing page)
Pottery, CG130
Atelier Vierkant
Clay
H: 128cm (51in)
W (base): 30cm (11¾in)
W (top): 39cm (15⅜in)
Atelier Vierkant, Belgium
www.ateliervierkant.com

(above)
Concrete planter, Modernist
Kathy Dalwood
Concrete
H: 28cm (11in)
W: 28cm (11in)
L: 28cm (11in)
Kathy Dalwood, UK
www.kathydalwood.com

(below)
Planter, Reuse Planter (5 Gallon Triple)
Loll Designs
100% post-consumer recycled plastic
H: 43cm (17in)
W: 102.2cm (40¼in)
D: 35cm (13¾in)
Loll Designs, US
www.lolldesigns.com

(above)
Modular planter/ trellis system, cElements
Michael Hilgers
Galvanized and powder-coated steel
H: 75cm (29in)
W: 75cm (29in)
D: 15cm (5⅞in)
Rephorm, Germany
www.rephorm.de

(below)
Planter, Stainless Steel Planter
Tornado
Stainless steel
H: 60cm (23in)
W: 60cm (23in)
Tornado, UK
www.tornado.co.uk

(left)
Planter, Wing
Michael Koenig
Powder-coated
aluminium
H: 69cm (27in)
W: 60cm (23in)
L: 125cm (49in)
Flora Wilh. Förster
GmbH & Co. KG,
Germany
www.flora-online.de

(above)
Planter, Re-Trouvé
Patricia Urquiola
Painted pre-galvanized
steel, terracotta
H: 105cm (41in)
Diam: 72cm (28in)
Emu Group SpA, Italy
www.emu.it

(right)
Pot, Rising Pots
Stefan Schöning
Porcelain, polyester,
terracotta
H (frames): 35, 65,
or 123cm (13¾,
25 or 48in)
H (pots): 30 or 60
(11¾ or 23in)
Diam (frame):
100cm (39in)
Diam (pot):
100cm (39in)
Domani Ltd, Belgium
www.domani.be

(left)
Pot, Hole Pot
Luisa Bocchietto
Polyethylene
H: 66cm (26in)
Diam: 66cm (26in)
Serralunga srl, Italy
www.serralunga.com

(above and right)
**Planter, The Retro
Bullet Planter**™
Hip Haven
Moulded fibreglass,
powder-coated steel
H: 41, 59 or 77cm
(16, 23 or 30in)
W: 41cm (16in)
D: 30cm (12in)
Hip Haven, Inc, US
www.hiphaven.com

(right)
**Flower pot,
Uve Aigua**
Studio Vondom
Low-density,
linear polythene
H: 80cm (31in)
W: 40cm (15¾in)
L: 120cm (47in)
Vondom, Spain
www.vondom.com

(above)
Pot, Tambo
Luca Nichetto
H: 73cm (28in)
W: 75cm (29in)
Plust Collection, Italy
www.plust.com

(above)
Planters, Sahara
Pablo Gironés
Polyethylene with gloss
lacquered finish
Various dimensions
Gandia Blasco SA, Spain
www.gandiablasco.com

(above)
**Pots collection,
Missed Tree**
Jean-Marie Massaud
Polyethylene
H: 159 or 200cm
(63 or 78in)
W: 42cm (16½in)
Serralunga srl, Italy
www.serralunga.com

(right)
Pot, Flow
Zaha Hadid
Polyethylene
H: 120, 200cm
(47, 78in)
W: 117 or 146cm
(46 or 57in)
Serralunga srl, Italy
www.serralunga.com

(left)
**Vase, Saving/
Space/Vase**
JVLT/JoeVelluto
Polyethylene
Diam: 57cm (22in)
Plust Collection, Italy
www.plust.com

(right)
Planter, Aladin
Patrick Schöni
Fibre cement
H: 59, 73 or 87cm
(23, 28 or 34in)
Diam: 112, 138
or 165cm
(44, 54 or 65in)
Eternit AG, Switzerland
www.eternit.ch

(right)
**Vase/planter,
Bubble Vase**
Erwin Vahlenkamp
Fibreglass-reinforced
polyester
H: 80 or 120cm
(31 or 47in)
Diam: 50cm (19in)
EGO² BV, the
Netherlands
www.ego2.com

(left)
**Green wall/living
wall/vertical garden/
wall planter,
Wally Pockets**
Miguel Nelson
Breathable felt and
built-in moisture barrier
H: 38cm (15in)
W: 61, 154 or
284.5cm (24,
61 or 112in)
Woolly Pocket
Gardening
Company, US
www.woollypocket.com

(above)
**Planters, Bespoke
Stainless Steel Planters**
Tills Innovations
Stainless steel
Bespoke sizes
Tills Innovations Ltd, UK
www.tills-innovations.com

(above)
**Flowerpot,
Pot-au-Mur**
Nicolas Le Moigne
Polypropylene
H: 90cm (35in)
W: 45cm (17¾in)
D: 45cm (17¾in)
Serralunga srl, Italy
www.serralunga.com

(right)
**Pot system, Family
Pot Suspension**
Mauro Canfori
Teralite, lacquered
metal
H: 206cm (81in)
W: 56cm (22in)
Teracrea srl, Italy
www.teracrea.com

(above and below)
**Modular planter,
Balconcino**
Sebastian Bergne
High-pressure
laminates
H: 165cm (65in)
W: 80cm (31in)
D: 38cm (15in)
Teracrea srl, Italy
www.teracrea.com

(above)
Planter, Dotti Planter
Peter McLisky
Powder-coated steel
H: 40cm (15¾in)
W: 40cm (15¾in)
D: 40cm (15¾in)
Peter Mclisky
Sculpture, Australia
www.petermclisky.
com.au

(above)
**Modular planters,
Rock Garden**
Alain Gilles
Rotation-moulded
low-density
polyethylene
H: 37.3cm (14⅝in)
W: 43.1cm (16⅞in)
L: 51.2cm (20in)
Qui est Paul?, France
www.qui-est-paul.com

(above)
**Modular flower
planters, Shift**
Rainer Mutsch
Cellulose-based Eternit
concrete panels
Small: 47 x 87 x 40cm
(18½ x 34 x 15¾in)
Medium:
45 x 72 x 55cm
(17¾ x 28 x 21in)
Large: 25 x 80 x 70cm
(9⅞ x 31 x 27in)
Eternit Werke L.
Hatschek AG, Austria
www.eternit.at

(right)
**Stool and,
if overturned,
ice bucket, Drink**
Jorge Nàjera
Polyethylene
H: 75cm (29in)
Diam: 45cm
(17¾in)
Slide srl, Italy
www.slidedesign.it

(left)
Bowl/planter, Pond bowl
Erwin Vahlenkamp
Fibreglass-reinforced polyester
H: 10cm, 15 cm and 20cm
(3⅞in, 5⅞in and 7⅞in)
Diam: 50cm, 75cm and 100cm
(19in, 29in and 39in)
EGO² BV, the Netherlands
www.ego2.com

(below)
Vase, Delta
Benedetto Fasciana
Cor-ten, cast iron, satin stainless steel
H: from 98cm (38in)
Diam (lower base): from 27.4cm (10⅝in)
Diam (upper base): from 50cm (19in)
De Castelli, Italy
www.decastelli.com

(above)
Planter, Relax!
Stauffacher Benz
Fibre cement
H: 12cm (4¾in)
W: 76cm (29in)
L: 189cm (74in)
Eternit AG, Switzerland
www.eternit.ch

(right)
Multipurpose container, Sweet Cake
Beerd van Stokkum
Indestructible plastic
H: 27cm (10⅝in)
Diam (top): 70cm (27in)
Beerd van Stokkum, the Netherlands
www.beerdvanstokkum.com

(above)
**Planter for
balcony railings,
Steckling Cube**
Michael Hilgers
Recyclable
polyethylene
H: 30cm (11¾in)
W: 30cm (11¾in)
D: 30cm (11¾in)
Rephorm, Germany
www.rephorm.de

(above)
Pot, Pot Cavalier
Rafaële David,
Géraldine Hetzel
Flax fibres, resin
H: 26cm (10¼in)
W: 26cm (10¼in)
az&mut, France
www.az-et-mut.fr

(above)
Wall planter, Tetris
Jamie Dunstan,
PSI Nurseries
Stainless steel, powder
coat colour finish
Various dimensions,
all constructed from
15 x 15cm (5⅞ x 5⅞in)
box section
stainless steel
S3i Ltd – Stainless
Steel Solutions, UK
www.s3i.co.uk

(left)
Flower box, Sunset
Michael Koenig
Aluminium sheet
metal, powder-
coated anthracite and
anthracite/orange
with plastic insert
H: 21cm (8¼in)
W: 16cm (6¼in)
L: 60, 80 or 100cm
(23, 31 or39in)
Flora Wilh. Förster
GmbH & Co. KG,
Germany
www.flora-online.de

Michael Hilgers

The design aesthetic of the balcony or roof terrace should be no different to the contemporary interior, but you will know only too well if you have either or both that it is still hard to find contemporary designs for these areas. This subject so preoccupied the German product designer Michael Hilgers of Rephorm that he developed a range of designs for just such small, awkward spaces – or, to quote his company slogan, "solutions for the interface between private interior and exterior space." Hilgers was initially surprised by the disparity between the look of interiors and exteriors. "A lot of people," he says, "have Alessi products and suchlike inside their homes but they have fake rustic stuff outside – why?" What surprised him more was that these extremes of taste, as Hilgers notes, "are only divided by window glass".

Based in Berlin, Hilgers trained initially as an architect, "but I decided I didn't want to build houses, I wanted to work on a smaller scale, so I returned to my former training as a joiner and started to design products." He began with furniture – Hilgers had designed and independently produced Dialounge pair chair (a prototype in wood) and showed it at Cologne Furniture Fair. Two things happened at this fair that would change his direction. Firstly, people told him the chair would be good as an outdoor product made in plastic, and this led him to investigate rotomoulding (or rotational moulding), a fast-growing sector of the plastics industry with low tooling costs, making it a much more cost-effective way of manufacturing. And, secondly, Hilgers also became aware of the dearth of well-designed outdoor products – especially for small spaces like balconies and terraces. "So the way was prepared," he says, "as a designer you always look for niches in the market."

Hilgers is an independent designer, producing products that combine ingenuity with playfulness and functionality. Take Steckling (see opposite) a water-resistant, polyethylene flower pot that straddles the balcony railings securely, or Vertvert, a tiered planter system that allows you to grow the maximum produce in the minimum space. Then there's Rohrspatz (see right), a charming anthropomorphic ashtray whose bird-like talons clutch the balcony railings, or Sling (see p.145), a balcony light with a simple, twisted organic stem that attaches itself to the railings, as securely as a vine.

This man is the answer to many frustrated balcony gardeners' dreams. Most of Hilgers' products require no securing, and in some countries such as Sweden, where there are laws to prevent you hanging pots over the railings, Hilgers' planters are perfectly legal.

Hilgers agrees that there seems to be a huge increase of interest in gardening in general and the greening of urban spaces in particular. "I live in Berlin," he says, "and there's a very high density of concrete and stone and everybody's looking to the countryside around Berlin, but not everyone can afford to buy a house in the country, so balconies, terraces and so forth become scaled-down versions of nature. Everything is personalized these days, you can personalize your iPhone, your car, so why not your balcony?"

Hilgers gets ideas for his products in a novel way. "I walk through the street and keep my head up," he says. "There are a lot of self-made structures which are sometimes very inspiring, because there is a lack of products for balconies, people tend to improvise – there are not a lot of professional designers working in this area. In Berlin there are 4,000-5,000 designers and in London I think there are about the same number, but no one seems to have thought much about this topic and it's so close to us – everybody has it in their sights."

Hilgers' most recent project is a small collection of low-budget items made in China. "I think," he smiles, "we might be at the beginning of more balcony democracy." He has also been turning his attention to the interior – he talks about ideas for (just-add-water) indoor herb gardens and magnetized herb containers that attach to your fridge. Hilgers' products are attracting a young design-conscious audience rather than budding horticulturalists, but perhaps, indirectly, he is nurturing gardeners of the future.

(above)
Window box/ planter, Herb
Michael Hilgers
Recyclable polyethylene
H: 21cm (8¼in)
W: 50cm (19in)
D: 21cm (8¼in)
Rephorm, Germany
www.rephorm.de

(below)
Ashtray for balcony railings, Rohrspatz
Michael Hilgers
Powder-coated steel, stainless steel
Diam: 12cm (4¾in)
Rephorm, Germany
www.rephorm.de

(facing page)
Watering can, Camilla
Koziol Werksdesign
Polypropylene
H: 40cm (15¾in)
W: 42cm (16½in)
D: 16cm (6¼in)
Koziol, Germany
www.koziol.de

(above)
**Watering can,
Bo-tanica**
Denis Santachiara
Polyethylene
H: 55cm (21in)
W: 37cm (14⅜in)
Serralunga srl, Italy
www.serralunga.com

(left)
Watering can, 1.5 L
Pascal Charmolu
Stainless steel, silicone
H: 31cm (12¼in)
Diam: 8cm (3⅛in)
Born in Sweden,
Sweden
www.borninsweden.se

(above)
Watering can, 7.5 L
Pascal Charmolu
Recyclable
polypropylene,
stainless steel
H: 56cm (22in)
Diam (base):
20cm (7⅞in)
Born in Sweden,
Sweden
www.borninsweden.se

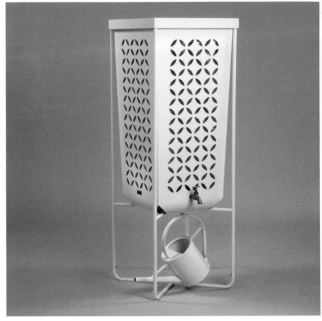

(left)
**Rainwater tank,
Rainwater HOG**
Sally Dominguez
Low-density
polyethylene
H: 180cm (71in)
W: 51cm (20in)
D: 24cm (9½in)
Rainwater HOG LLC, US
www.rainwaterhog.com

(above)
**Rain catcher/barrel,
RC-1 Rain Collector**
Leo Corrales,
Jenny Lemieux
Powder-coated
steel, phthalate-free
tarpaulin bladder,
brass, stainless steel
H: 145cm (57in)
W: 51cm (20in)
D: 51cm (20in)
Hero Design
Lab Inc., Canada
www.hero-365.com

(above)
Plant support, Tutrix
Rafaële David,
Géraldine Hetzel
Hemp, pp
H: 27cm (10⅝in)
az&mut, France
www.az-et-mut.fr

(right)
**Rainwater tank,
Lumi™**
Full Tank
Polyethylene,
Plexiglas®,
LEDs
H: 132cm (52in)
W: 72cm (28in)
Full Tank, Australia
www.fulltank.com.au

(above)
**Planter with
trellis, Air**
Michael Koenig
Powder-coated
aluminium
H: 182cm (72in)
W: 55cm (21in)
D: 33cm (13in)
Flora Wilh. Förster
GmbH & Co. KG,
Germany
www.flora-online.de

(right)
**Rainwater
harvester, Cista**
Moss Sund
and Fig Forty
Stainless steel, TPO, ivy
H: 240cm (94in)
W: 50cm (19in)
D: 35cm (13¾in)
Moss Sund, Canada
www.mosssund.com

Water
features

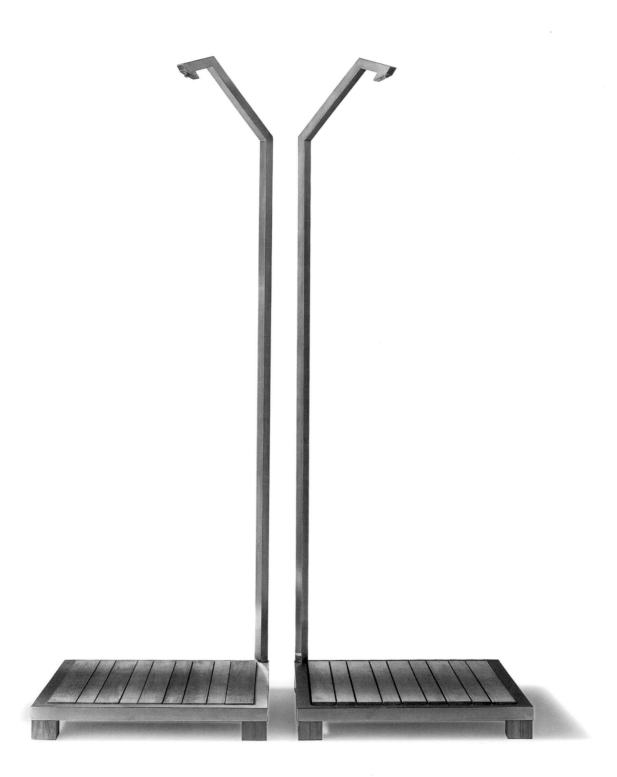

(above)
**Water feature/
fountain, Blue
Fountain**
Neil Wilkin
Hand-crafted
solid blue glass,
stainless steel
H (approx.):
100cm (39in)
Diam: 100cm (39in)
Neil Wilkin, UK
and Australia
www.neilwilkin.com

(above)
**Floating fountain,
Air Flo LM**
OASE GmbH
Plastic, stainless steel
H: 70cm (27in)
Diam: 115cm (45in)
OASE GmbH, Germany
www.oase-livingwater.com

(right)
**Water sculpture,
Coanda**
William Pye
Polished stainless steel
H: 190cm (74in)
Diam: 125cm (49in)
William Pye, UK
www.williampye.com

(left)
**Water sculpture,
Coracle**
William Pye
Bronze/stainless steel
W: 120cm (47in)
L: 240cm (94in)
William Pye, UK
www.williampye.com

(above)
**Water sculpture,
Meniscus**
William Pye
Polished stainless
steel/bronze
Diam: 200cm (78in)
William Pye, UK
www.williampye.com

(right)
**Submersible exterior
light, Float Rope**
Sam Wise
Polyethylene,
aluminium,
Incandescent
bulb or LED
L: up to 100m (328ft)
Diam: 6.5 or 11cm
(2⅝ or 4⅜in)
Wise1design, UK
www.wise1design.com

(above)
**Modular/Planter/
Bench/Fountain
system, Bench/
Fountain/Planter**
Campania International
Cast stone
H: 38cm (15in)
W: 43cm (17in)
L: 566cm (223in)
Campania
International Inc, US
www.campania
international.com

(left)
Fountain, Echo Fountain
Campania International
Cast stone
H: 163cm (64in)
W: 41cm (16in)
L: 36cm(14in)
Campania
International, Inc, US
www.campania
international.com

(above)
Glass pavilion
Christopher Bradley-
Hole Landscape
Toughened glass
H: 300cm (118in)
W: 300cm (118in)
I: 300cm (118in)
Firman Glass, UK
www.firmanglass.com
www.christopher
bradley-hole.co.uk

(left)
Water feature,
Double Waterwall
Elena Colombo
Water jet-cut
cor-ten steel
H: 244cm (96in)
L: 366cm (144in)
Colombo Construction
Corp, US
www.firefeatures.com

(above)
Water feature,
Paving Candle Jets
Andrew Ewing
Acero Limestone,
stainless steel, water,
fibre optics
W: 180cm (70in)
L: 180cm (70in)
Andrew Ewing Design,
UK
www.andrewewing.co.uk

(left)
**Straight water
wall complete
with extended
feature sides,
Bespoke
Water Feature**
GA Waterfeatures
Grade 316 mirror-
polished stainless steel,
grade 316 brushed
stainless steel
H: 220cm (86in)
W: 180cm (70in)
The Garden
Builders, UK
www.gardenbuilders.co.uk
www.gawaterfeatures.co.uk

(right)
**Wavy water wall
feature with curving
lower tank, Bespoke
Water Feature**
GA Waterfeatures
Grade 316 mirror-
polished stainless steel,
grade 316 brushed
stainless steel
H: 230cm (90in)
W: 120cm (47in)
The Garden
Builders, UK
www.gardenbuilders.co.uk
www.gawater
features.co.uk

(right)
**Pool and garden,
Cedarhurst Pool
and Garden**
John Davis, Sarah
Munster
Concrete
W (pool): 23cm (9in)
L (pool): 99cm (39in)
Architecture and
Gardens, US
www.architecture
andgardens.net

(below)
Water feature, Identify
Andy Sturgeon
Landscape &
Garden Design
Stone, wood
The Garden
Builders, UK
www.gardenbuilders.co.uk

(right)
**Water feature,
Dulwich Town Garden**
Andy Sturgeon
Landscape &
Garden Design
Concrete blocks,
stainless steel
H: 140cm (55in)
W: 550cm (217in)
The Garden
Builders, UK
www.gardenbuilders.co.uk

(right)
**Courtyard garden,
Modernist Courtyard
with Water Feature**
Charlotte Rowe
Guido Blue Portuguese
limestone, Acero
Portuguese limestone
W: 900cm (354in)
D (at its widest point):
700cm (275in)
Charlotte Rowe
Garden Design, UK
www.charlotterowe.com

(above)
**Water feature,
Firespill**
Elena Colombo
Steel or bronze
W: 91cm (35in)
L: 244cm (96in)
Colombo Construction
Corp, US
www.firefeatures.com

(right)
**Fountain, Negative
Edge Fountain**
Mesa
Stainless steel,
natural slate
H: 107cm (42in)
W (upper):
94cm (37in)
W (lower):
91cm (36in)
L (upper basin):
732cm (288in)
L (lower basin):
853cm (336in)
D (upper):
40.6cm (16in)
D (lower): 38cm (15in)
Mesa, US
www.mesadesign
group.com

(facing page)
**Pool, Natural
Swimming Pool**
Gartenart Natural
Swimming Ponds
W: 5m (16½ft)
L: 16m (52½ft)
Gartenart Natural
Swimming Ponds, UK
www.gartenart.co.uk

(above)
**Water feature
and pond, Docklands
Roof Garden**
Andy Sturgeon
Landscape &
Garden Design
Glass, wood, stones
The Garden
Builders, UK
www.gardenbuilders.co.uk

(right)
**Water feature,
Water Feature Rill**
Andy Sturgeon
Landscape &
Garden Design
Stone, wood
The Garden
Builders, UK
www.gardenbuilders.co.uk

(above)
**Natural swimming
pool, Type 4
'Compact
Planted' Pool**
Clear Water Revival
PVC, concrete,
river cobbles
Diam (swimming area):
400cm (157in)
Clear Water Revival, UK
www.clear-water-
revival.com

(above)
**Pool, Natural
Swimming Pool**
Gartenart Natural
Swimming Ponds
W: 7m (23ft)
L: 15.8m (52ft)
Gartenart Natural
Swimming Ponds, UK
www.gartenart.co.uk

(right)
**Water sculpture,
Shimmer**
William Pye
Polished stainless steel
W: 149.2cm (59in)
L: 399.6cm (157in)
William Pye, UK
www.williampye.com

Ulf Nordfjell

Ulf Nordfjell is still bathing in the golden light of success when I talk to him – he was recently awarded Gold and Best in Show for the Daily Telegraph Garden at Chelsea Flower Show, London, 2009. The Stockholm-based landscape architect's winning design combined the clean lines of Swedish Modernism with the charm of the English cottage garden. This is a clever fusion as the austerity of Modernism is softened, while the often blousy exuberance of the cottage garden landscape is calmed and refined. It is the merging of these two distinct styles that give Nordfjell's work such originality.

"There is an enormous influence and impact from nature and the British landscape in my designs," he says, "because I take things from the landscape all the time and put them in a modern setting." He cites Hidcote and Sissinghurst as examples of gardens he finds inspirational. Of Sissinghurst, with its ten distinct garden rooms, Nordfjell says, "You look through the holes in the hedges and you see all these different rooms, you see something new every time you visit, and that to me is what gardening is all about."

"I'm obsessed by the theatre too." he says. citing another source of inspiration. "I have always tried to mimic the theatre in my garden designs because of its ability to transport your mind elsewhere – the suspension of disbelief."

For Nordfjell the garden is a celebration of nature and he frequently introduces it, literally, into his schemes. As he says, "I often put wild plants into minimalist settings, the lingonberry for example, is a plant you would never notice much in nature, but when you present it in formal settings it looks quite exquisite. It's also my way of saying 'nature is without competition.'"

Nordfjell's palette is subtle, a cool northern combination of blues, whites and greys, mingling grasses with fluffy seedheads for texture with plants such as campanula and violets for flashes of colour. For hard landscaping he uses what he calls "Swedish materials" – durable commodities such as wood, granite, steel and glass that will withstand the extreme Scandinavian winter. Nordfjell's gardens are places of quiet retreat where sights, sounds and senses are heightened, and one where water is always a key element.

Water is of particular importance to Nordfjell and he uses it frequently. What qualities does water possess that attracts him to it? "Water," he replies, "is life here in Scandinavia. I would say only Britain and Scandinavia has enough water, the rest of the world is suffering from a lack of it. Today our relationship is much more ecological than it was in the '60s. Today we take things out of the water rather than putting things in it." Water also relates to another aspect of his work: "Movement," says Nordfjell, "is essential to my designs. I really want the water to move so I want bubbles in it, because it's the air that gives you the feeling that the water is alive. It's also the air that makes the water glitter when the sunlight hits it. My view of water may be a little sentimental but that's because when I was growing up I spent the summers close to the river, an enormous stretch of running water. Some people, I would say, are related to the sea, some are related to the lakes, and I am related to the river. This is why I put all this running water into my gardens."

Nordfjell's background is of particular relevance in shaping his design concept. He has made pottery since he was 14 and his understanding of the making process, and of form, scale and texture, has informed the range of garden objects and furniture he has designed and developed with his own company Lunab. Nordfjell is also a qualified botanist, biologist and chemist. "To begin with," he says, "I didn't understand how to use this background in my landscaping but it has become clearer in the last six or seven years or so, both in terms of botany and in terms of my ecological thinking, and it's become much clearer in my design now."

Gardening for Nordfjell is also about getting your hands dirty, as he explains. "The garden should be a combination of pleasure and doing the maintenance – maintenance is an integral part of experiencing that pleasure, rather than worrying about where to put the grill... We live in a world controlled by computers, but growing plants has nothing to do with anything technical, it's just about using your hands and your heart and that's why everyone's into growing now."

(above)
**Garden design
with water feature**
Paul Dracott
Garden Design
Rendered walls,
metal screening,
cedar decking
The Garden
Builders, UK
www.gardenbuilders.co.uk

(left)
**Infinity edge
swimming pool,
Swimming Pool in
Thousand Oaks,
California**
Girvin Associates, Inc.
Landscape Architects
Pebbletec pool surface
and stone deck
W: 21.34m (70ft)
L: 9.14m (30ft)
D: 2.13m (7ft)
Girvin Associates,
Inc Landscape
Architects, US
www.girvinassoc.net

(right)
**Pool, California
Residence Pool**
Dufner Heighes Inc.
Kashmere cleft slate
(patio), Bisazza
glass mosaic tile
(pool interior)
W: 6.1m (20ft)
L: 13.7m (45ft)
Dufner Heighes
Inc, US
www.dufnerheighes.com

(left)
**Natural swimming
pool, Type 3
'Compact
Planted' pool**
Simon Ovenstone
PVC, concrete,
river cobbles
Surface area: 25–70m²
(269–753ft²)
Clear Water Revival, UK
www.clear-water-
revival.com

(right)
**Swimming pool
surrounded by lawn
with fountain jets set
into the pool coping**
Frederika Moller
Bluestone pool
coping, Tahoe blue
pool plaster colour
W: 5.8m (19ft)
L: 17.7m (58ft)
Frederika Moller
Landscape
Architect, US
www.fmland.net

(right)
Pool area, Queens Park Pool
CplusC
Pergola structure: Jarrah and western red cedar
Deck: blue gum
Pool coping: Burmese teak.
W (pool): 300cm (118in)
L (pool): 800cm (315in)
CplusC, Australia
www.cplusc.com.au

(above)
Garden design with swimming pool, Mediterranean Villa
Catherine Heatherington
Local stone for walls, local limestone and slate paving
W (pool): 600cm (236in)
L (pool): 1200cm (472in)
Catherine Heatherington Designs, UK
www.chdesigns.co.uk

(right)
Landscaped Pool
Secret Gardens of Sydney
Stone, timber, bamboo
W (pool): 300cm (118in)
L (pool): 900cm (354in)
Secret Gardens of Sydney, Australia
www.secret gardens.com.au

(above and left)
**Garden design
with pool**
Dan Gayfer
(landscape architect)
Concrete, glass
W: 300cm (118in)
L: 430cm (169in)
Out From The
Blue, Australia
www.outfromtheblue.
com.au

(right)
**Hydrospa,
Seaside 640**
Teuco
High-grade methacrylate
W: 225cm (88in)
L: 258cm (102in)
Teuco, Italy
www.teuco.com

(left)
Spa
Yves
Pertosa Group
Resin with
mineral powders
H: 101–104cm
(40–41in)
W: 209cm (82in)
L: 360cm (141in)
D: 82cm (32in)
Pertosa Group, France
www.sensoriel-spa.com

(above)
**Garden design
with pool**
Dan Gayfer
(landscape architect)
Concrete, glass,
stainless steel
W: 2.3m (7½ft)
L: 12.9m (42ft)
Out From The Blue,
Australia
www.outfromtheblue.
com.au

(above)
**Garden design
with pool**
Dan Gayfer
(landscape architect)
Concrete, ceramic
W: 450cm (177in)
L: 800cm (315in)
Out From The
Blue, Australia
www.outfromtheblue.
com.au

(left)
**Pool, Faraway
Minipool**
Ludovica+Roberto
Palomba
Fibreglass
H: 100cm (39in)
W: 261cm (103in)
L: 456cm (183in)
Kos, Italy
www.kositalia.com

(above)
Pool, Blue Moon Pool
Jochen Schmiddem
Sanitary acrylic,
wooden teak,
stainless steel, chrome
Underwater, coloured
lighting controlled
by a water-resistant
remote control
H: 70.5cm (28in)
W: 140 or 180cm
(55 or 70in)
L: 140 or 180cm
(55 or 70in)
D: 56cm (22in)
Duravit, Germany
www.duravit.com

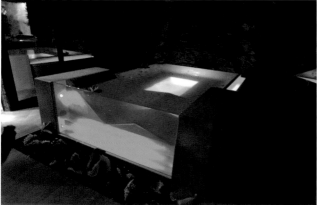
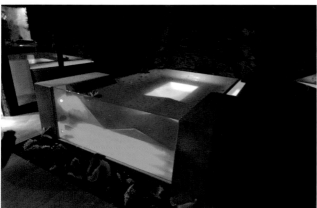

(above)
Spa, Infinéa
Pertosa Group
Resin with
mineral powders
H: 103cm (40½in)
W: 220cm (86in)
L: 288cm (113in)
D: 82cm (32in)
Pertosa Group, France
www.sensoriel-spa.com

(right)
Bath tub, Napali Tub
Mark Rogero
Concrete
H: 64cm (25in)
W: 152cm (60in)
D: 107cm (42in)
Concreteworks, US
www.concreteworks.com

(above)
**Multipurpose pool
(swimming against
current, dynamic
massage, whirlpool),
Mini-Water**
Aquilus
Composite framework
W: 214cm (84in)
L: 402cm (157in)
Aquilus, France
www.aquilus-piscine.com
www.aquilus-spas.com

(above)
**Hydrospa,
Mirror 630**
Teuco
High-grade
methacrylate
W: 235cm (92in)
L: 300cm (118in)
Teuco, Italy
www.teuco.com

(left)
Spa, Cube
Pertosa Group
Resin with
mineral powders
H: 101cm to 104cm
(40in to 41in)
W: 209cm (82in)
L: 209cm (82in)
D: 82cm (32in)
Pertosa Group, France
www.sensoriel-spa.com

(left)
**Spa, Spa for
Dolomites House**
JM Architecture
Ipê wood, steel
D: (hot tub):
98cm (38in)
Diam (hot tub):
237cm (93in)
JM Architecture, Italy
www.jma.it

(above)
**Portable wood-fired
hot tub, Dutchtub**
Floris Schoonderbeek
Polyfibre, stainless steel
H: 84cm (33in)
W: 170cm (67in)
L: 260cm (102in)
Dutchtub, the
Netherlands
www.dutchtub.com

(below)
Spa, Copper Spa
Diamond Spas
Copper
W: 183cm (72in)
L: 229cm (90in)
D: 91cm (36in)
Diamond Spas, US
www.diamondspas.com

(left)
**Overflow bathtub,
Pond**
Käsch
Acrylic,
polyester, wood
Power LED colour light
H: 65cm (25in)
W: 120, 130
or 150cm
(47, 51 or 59in)
L: 200, 210 or 220cm
(78, 82 or 86in)
D: 50cm (19½in)
Käsch, Germany
www.kaesch.biz

(above)
**Overflow bathtub,
Lake**
Käsch
Acrylic, polyester,
stone, cement,
glass, aluminium
Power LED colour light
H: 65cm (25in)
W: 130cm (51in)
L: 220cm (86in)
D: 50cm (19½in)
Käsch, Germany
www.kaesch.biz

(left)
**Tub/Padded lounger,
Duravit Sundeck**
EOOS Design Group
Sanitary acrylic, wood
Underwater, coloured
lighting controlled
by water-resistant
remote control
H: 64cm (25in)
W: 140cm (55in)
L: 210cm (82in)
D: 47cm (18½in)
Duravit, Germany
www.duravit.com

(above)
**Spa, Flore
Pertosa Group**
Resin with
mineral powders
H: 103cm to 104cm
(40½in to 41in)
W: 235cm (92in)
L: 260cm (102in)
D: 85cm (33in)
Pertosa Group, France
www.sensoriel-spa.com

(facing page)
**Bathtub,
Hinoki Cypress**
Ryu Kosaka
Wood
H: 63cm (24in)
Diam: 181.5cm
(71in)
Furo, Japan
www.furo.co.jp

(above)
**Bathtub, Urushi
Lacquer**
Yukio Hashimoto
Lacquer
H: 55cm (21in)
W: 90.5cm (35in)
L: 179cm (70in)
Furo, Japan
www.furo.co.jp

(right)
**Hot tub with
42-inch TV, DVD,
CD and speakers and
adjustable therapy
system seat,
Galaxy 49**
Cal Spas
Smooth acrylic shell
LED lighting
H: 236cm (93in)
W: 100cm (39½in)
L: 236cm (93in)
Cal Spas, US
www.calspas.com

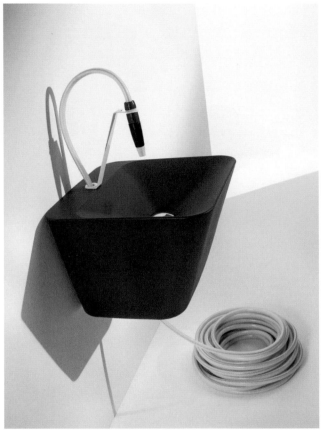

(above)
Bathtub, Light LTT
Jan Puylaert
100% recyclable
polyethylene
H: 60cm (23in)
W: 85cm (33in)
L: 175cm (68in)
D: 45cm (17¾in)
Wet, Italy
www.wet.co.it

(above)
Washbasin, Simplex
Martín Ruiz de Azúa,
Gerard Moliné
Plastic
H: 38cm (15in)
W: 50cm (19in)
D: 50cm (19in)
Cosmic, Spain
www.icosmic.com

(left)
**Portable sink,
Hughie Sink**
Ian Alexander
Recycled
polypropylene plastic
H: 12cm (4¾in)
W: 38cm (15in)
L: 44cm (17⅜in)
Hughie Products,
Australia
www.hughie.com.au

Spa, Evasion
Pertosa Group
Resin with
mineral powders
H: 101cm to 104cm
(40in to 41in)
W: 209cm (82in)
L: 260cm (102in)
D: 82cm (32in)
Pertosa Group, France
www.sensoriel-spa.com

(above)
**Outdoor shower,
Dyno**
Moredesign
Polyethylene,
chrome-plated
brass, ABS
H: 229cm (90in)
W: 38cm (15in)
D: 86cm (33in)
Myyour, Italy
www.myyour.eu

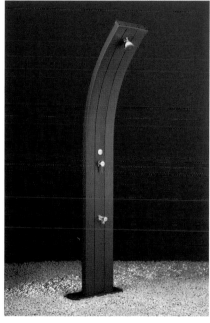

(above)
**Solar shower,
DADA D 320**
Jean Rusconi
Aluminium
H: 235cm (92in)
W: 30cm (11¾in)
D: 18cm (7⅛in)
Arkema, Italy
www.arkemadesign.com

(right)
**Outdoor shower,
Ocean**
Dieter Peischl
Acid-resistant
stainless steel
H: 236cm (92in)
W: 15cm (5⅞in)
D: 50cm (19in)
Designerzeit, Austria
www.designerzeit.com

(above)
**Mobile outdoor
shower, Cascade**
Jean-Pierre Galeyn
Galvanized steel,
acacia wood, nylon
H: 220cm (86in)
W: 70cm (27in)
L: 70cm (27in)
Tradewinds, Belgium
www.trade-winds.be

(above)
**Outdoor shower,
Tolda (art. 983)**
Sante Martinuzzi
Stainless steel, teak
wood
H: 230cm (90in)
W: 76cm (29in)
TPL srl, Italy
www.teakparkline.it

(right)
Shower, Doccia
Adalberto Mestre
Stainless steel
H: 215cm (84in)
L: 40cm (15¾in)
Dimensione
Disegno srl, Italy
www.dimensionedisegno.it

(left)
Shower, Waterfall
Shower
Mark Suensilpong
Teak, stainless steel
H: 218cm (86in)
W: 100cm (39in)
D: 105cm (41in)
Jane Hamley Wells, US
www.janehamleywells.com

(above)
Outdoor shower,
AquaBambù
Bossini Outdoor
Shower Systems
Stainless steel
H: 211cm (83in)
Bossini SpA, Italy
www.bossini.it

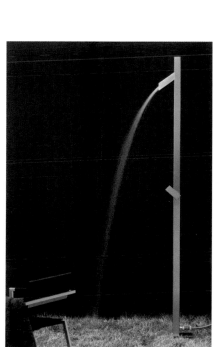

(above)
Garden shower,
Under the Tree
Michael Sieger
Stainless steel
H: 230cm (90in)
W: 39cm (15⅜in)
D: 11cm (4⅜in)
Conmoto, Germany
www.conmoto.com

(left)
Garden shower, UNO
Sebastian David
Büscher
Stainless steel
H: 220cm (86in)
W: 10cm (3⅞in)
D: 5cm (2in)
Conmoto, Germany
www.conmoto.com

(right)
Shower
Danny Venlet
Plastic, stainless steel
H: 11cm (4⅜in)
Diam: 78cm (30in)
Viteo Outdoors, Austria
www.viteo.at

(above)
Shower, EWD
Danny Venlet
Stainless steel
H: 210cm (82in)
Diam (plate): 40cm
(15¾in)
Coro, Italy
www.coroitalia.it

(right)
Shower, Khepri
Staubach & Kuckertz
Brushed stainless steel,
solid exotic wood
H: 240cm (94in)
W: 106cm (42in)
D: 106cm (42in)
Metalco, Italy
www.metalco.it

(right)
Shower, Silver Cascade Shower (Siena)
Manutti
Teak, stainless steel
H: 222cm (87in)
W: 90cm (35in)
L: 90cm (35in)
Manutti, Belgium
www.manutti.com

(above)
Free standing shower, Samurai
Newform Style and Design
Stainless steel
H: 253cm (100in)
Newform SpA, Italy
www.newform.it

(left)
Mobile outdoor shower, WellWell
Jean-Pierre Galeyn
Aluminium, acacia wood
H: 11cm (4⅜in)
W: 15cm (5⅞in)
L: 47cm (18½in)
Tradewinds, Belgium
www.trade-winds.be

Lighting

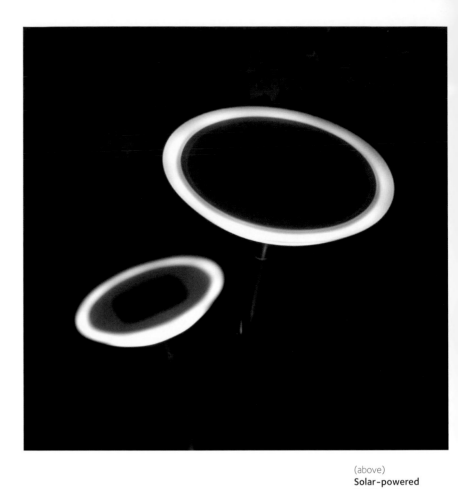

(above)
**Solar-powered
lighting, Corona**
Shane Kohatsu,
Emi Fujita
Powder-coated steel,
polycarbonate, TPU,
photo-voltaic panels
LED
H: 60–150cm
(23–59in)
W: 15cm (5⅞in)
D: 15cm (5⅞in)
Corona Solar Light, US
www.coronasolarlight.co

(left)
**Lamp,
Mamanonmama**
Francesco Sani
Stainless steel
TC-B 23W E27
or 6 LED x 1W
H: 50cm (19in)
W: 33cm (13in)
Menichetti Outdoor
Lighting, Italy
www.menichetti-srl.it

(left)
Light, Sky
Alfredo Häberli
Aluminium,
polycarbonate
Solar version: 8 x LED
high-efficiency
H: 16, 28 or 70cm
(6¼, 11 or 27in)
W: 20cm (7⅞in)
D: 20cm (7⅞in)
Luceplan, Italy
www.luceplan.com

(above)
Lamp, Amanita
Joan Verdugo
Aluminium
E27 15W FBT
H: 20cm (7⅞in)
Diam: 30cm (11¾in)
Marset, Spain
www.marset.com

(left)
Lamp, Tama
Isao Hosoe
Coloured ABS,
plastic polyethylene
1 x 60W max 230V
E27 or 1 x 23W max
230V E27 fluorescent
H: 42cm (16½in)
Diam: 36cm (14⅛in)
Valenti srl, Italy
www.valentiluce.it

(above)
Portable and adjustable light, Flexo
R. Fiorato, F. Pagliarini
Plastic, aluminium, stainless steel, glass
1 x max 23W/E27 compact fluorescent bulb
H: 33 or 30cm (13 or 11¾in)
Diam: 17.5cm (6⅞in)
Klewe – Performance In Lighting, Italy
www.pil-uk.com

(left)
Outdoor ground-recessed spotlight, Evoé
Marc Sadler
Aluminium, tempered striped glass, stainless steel
Halogen, fluorescent or LED
W: 24.8cm (9⅞in)
L: 27cm (10⅝in)
Artemide SpA, Italy
www.artemide.com

(above)
Light, Cobra
Kris Van Puyvelde
Stainless steel
1 x 1W Power LED
H: 60cm (23in)
W: 13cm (5⅛in)
Royal Botania, Belgium
www.royalbotania.com

(above)
Lamps, Panamá
Mario Ruiz
Aluminium
LED 6 x 1.2W
H: 45 or 65cm
(17 ¾ or 25in)
W: 37cm (14⅝in)
D: 13cm (5⅛in)
Metalarte SA, Spain
www.metalarte.com

(above)
**Lighting fixture,
Branch**
Rotorgroup for Modular
Lighting Instruments
Zytel, thermoplastics
LED 6W – CDMR
PAR30 – compact
fluorescence PAR30
H (one unit): 30.1cm
(11¾in) (can be stacked
up to 3 high)
Diam: 13cm (5⅛in)
Modular Lighting
Instruments, Belgium
www.supermodular.com

(left)
**Lamp,
OCO Garden Lamp**
Causas Externas
Painted aluminium,
high-quality recycled
and recyclable plastic
3 x LEDs
H: 33, 55, 99cm
(13, 21, 39in)
Diam: 15.5cm (6⅛in)
Santa & Cole, Spain
www.santacole.com

(above)
**Solar lamp, MIO
for Target Indoor &
Outdoor Solar Lamp**
Jaime Salm,
Roger C. Allen
Recycled plastic,
photocell, solar module
2 x LED
H: 16.5 or 30cm stem
(6½ or 12in stem)
Diam: 10cm (4in)
Target, US
www.target.com

(left)
Floor light, Toobo
Marco Merendi
Aluminium
1 x 35W GX10
(metal halide)
H: 220cm (86in)
Diam: 9.5cm (3¾in)
FontanaArte SpA, Italy
www.fontanaarte.it

(above)
Lighting, LED
Swinging Lightpole
Achim Jungbluth
Aluminium,
polycarbonate
8 LED, total 4W,
available with LEDs
in red, yellow, blue,
green or white
H: 150, 200 or 250cm
(59, 78 or 98in)
Diam: 4cm (1⅝in)
LFF Leuchten GmbH,
Germany
www.lff.de

(right)
Lighting, Koivu
Mike Radford
Birch ply or
stainless steel
80 spotlight/ E27
edison screw
H: 200–400cm
(78–157in)
Diam: 21–26cm
(8¼–10¼in)
4ddesigns, UK
www.4ddesigns.co.uk

(above left)
**Cordless illumination,
Havaleena Torch**
Tayo Design Studio
Aluminium, acrylic
1W LED
H (fixture):
6m (20ft)
Tayo Design Studio, US
www.tayodesign.com

(above)
Lamp, Lighttree
Alexander Lervik
Plastic, steel, fibre
Fibre optic with 150W
halogen projector
H: 150–400cm
(59–157in)
Diam: 100–200cm
(39–78in)
SAAS Instruments,
Finland
www.saas.fi

(above)
**Cordless illumination,
Havaleena Light
Bouquet**
Tayo Design Studio
Aluminium, acrylic
1W LED
H (fixture):
51cm (20in)
Tayo Design Studio, US
www.tayodesign.com

(right)
**Flexible post lamp,
LP Hint**
Helena Tatjana Eliason
Aluminium, acrylic,
polycarbonate
42W TC-TEL HF,
57W TC-TEL or
70W HIE/HIT
H: 300cm (118in)
Diam: 47.7cm
(18⅞in)
Louis Poulsen
Lighting, Sweden
www.louispoulsen.com

(right)
Lights, Antares
Chris Thornton
Coated metal
LEDs
H: 65–200cm
(25–78in)
Diam: 66, 85 or 200cm
(26, 33 or 78in)
Abraxus Lighting, UK
www.abraxuslighting.co.uk

(right)
Lamp, Sol-air
Nathalie Dewez
Carbon fibre, steel
Halogen lamp
max 1 x 50W
H: 250cm, 270cm
or 295cm (98,
106 or 116in)
W: 20cm (7⅞in)
Nathalie Dewez
Studio, Belgium
www.n-d.be

(left)
Lamp, Jerry
Luca Nichetto,
Carlo Tinti
Silicon
60W/220/240W
H: 2 /cm (10⅝in)
W: 16cm (6¼in)
D: 14cm (5½in)
Casamania, Italy
www.casamania.it

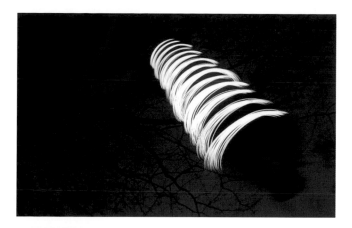

(above)
**Light, Firewinder®
– The Original
Windlight**
Tom Lawton
Acrylonitrile butadiene
styrene, acrylic,
stainless steel,
aluminium, mild steel,
copper, neodymium
iron boron rare earth
magnets (generator),
electronic components
surface-mounted LEDs
H: 65cm (25½in)
W: 18cm (7in)
The Firewinder
Company Limited, UK
www.firewinder.com

(left)
**Multi-purpose
lamp, Uto**
Lagranja Design for
Companies and Friends
Silicon rubber
1 x 60W incandescent
bulb/1 x 23W
fluorescent bulb
L: 320cm (126in)
Diam: 20cm (7⅛in)
Foscarini srl, Italy
www.foscarini.com

(right)
**Divider lamp/
sculptural lamp,
Snowhite**
Alberto Sánchez
White, painted
steel LEDs
H: 200cm (78in)
W: 40cm (15¾in)
L: 40 cm (15¾in)
Eneastudio, Spain
www.eneastudio.com

(facing page)
Lamp, Duna
Antonio Miró
Aluminium,
methacrylate
2 x E27 75W /
2 x 15W E27 FBT
H: 176.5cm (69in)
Diam: 43cm
(16⅞in)
Marset, Spain
www.marset.com

(right)
**Lamp, Boletus
Outside**
Jorge Pensi
Aluminium,
polyethylene
Fluorescent bulbs
2 x 36W (2G11)
H: 59cm (23in)
Diam: 51cm (20in)
B.Lux, Spain
www.grupoblux.com

(above)
Lamp, LUA (LU01)
Martín Azúa
White polyethylene
1 fluorescent compact
bulb: E27 – 1 x 20W
H: 50cm (19in)
Diam: 40cm
(15¾in)
Arturo Alvarez, Spain
www.arturo-alvarez.com

(left)
Lamps, Mora
Javier Mariscal
Polyethylene
Energy-saving
or LED RGB
H: 58 or 103 cm
(22 or 41in)
W: 28 or 33cm
(11 or 13in)
L: 28 or 33cm
(11 or 13in)
Vondom, Spain
www.vondom.com

(above)
**Floor lamp, Warm
Outdoor**
Enrico Franzolini
Polyethylene, metal
Fluorescent max
1 x 18W G24q-2
H: 160cm (63in)
W: 55cm (21in)
D: 60cm (23in)
Karboxx srl, Italy
www.karboxx.com

(right)
Lighted armchair, Translation
Alain Gilles
High-density polyethylene
Lamp 60W E27
H: 72.2cm (28in)
W: 74.7cm (29in)
D: 65.5cm (26in)
Qui est Paul?, France
www.qui-est-paul.com

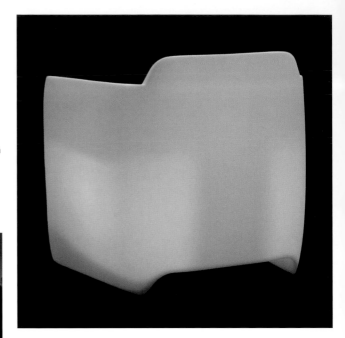

(above)
Lamp, Light Cube Mood
Wolfgang Pichler
Stainless steel, opal acrylic glass
RGB-LED circuit board, each with 24 LEDs / protection rating IP 65
H: 45cm (17¾in)
W: 40cm (15¾in)
L: 40cm (15¾in)
Viteo Outdoors, Austria
www.viteo.at

(right)
Seat and lamp, Bdlove Lamp
Ross Lovegrove
Rotation-moulded polyethylene
H: 300cm (118in)
W: 120cm (47in)
D: 141cm (56in)
Bd Barcelona, Spain
www.bdbarcelona.com

(right)
Cooler/atmosphere creator/garden lighting/bench, IceCube
Danny Venlet
Rotation-moulded polyethylene
Fitting IP65 for TL + 2 TL blue lights (2 x 36W)
H: 50cm (19in)
W: 50cm (19in)
L: 150cm (59in)
Extremis, Belgium
www.extremis.be

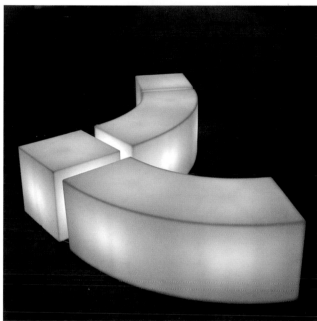

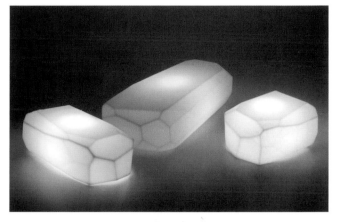

(above)
Occasional tables and seat with light, Meteor Light
Arik Levy
Polyethylene
1 fluorescent lamp energy saver
20W (E27)
H: 30, 32 or 34cm (11¾, 12⅝ or 13⅜in)
W: 50, 52 or 69 cm (19, 20 or 27in)
L: 57, 87 or 117cm (22, 34 or 46in)
Serralunga, Italy
www.serralunga.com

(above)
Luminous modular curved bench, Snake
Polyethylene
Energy-saving bulb: 2 x E27-15W
H: 43cm (16⅞in)
W: 123cm (48in)
D: 43cm (16⅞in)
Slide srl, Italy
www.slidedesign.it

(above and left)
Light, Harry and Harry Jardín
Porcuatro, Toni Pallejá
Stainless steel, polyethylene
1 x 23 max. (E-27 low energy)
H (Harry): 26cm (10¼in)
H (Harry Jardín): 34cm (13⅜in)
Diam: 48cm (18⅞in)
Carpyen S.L., Spain
www.carpyen.com

(right)
Wall lamp, Moo
Ove Rogne, Trond
Svendgård
Poly resin
Energy-saving bulbs
(E14 – 2 x 5W in
horns and E27 –
2 x 20W in head)
H: 75cm (29in)
W: 75cm (29in)
D: 57cm (22in)
Northern Lighting AS,
Norway
www.northernlighting.no

(above)
Lamp, Alien
Easy Outdoor
Constantin Wortmann,
Büro für Form
Polyethylene, steel
E27, ESL (energy-
saving lamps)
recommended
(normal bulbs:
medium size:
max 40W, XL size:
max 150W)
H: 66 or 11cm
(26 or 44 in)
Diam: 28 or 48cm
(11 or 18⅞in)
Next, Germany
www.next.de

(right)
Outdoor floor
and table lamp,
Atomium Outdoor
Hopf & Wortmann
Rotation-moulded
polyethylene
6 x E14 12W
Fluorescent
H: 52cm (20in)
W: 62cm (24in)
L: 57cm (22in)
Kundalini srl, Italy
www.kundalini.it

(above)
**Portable lamp,
Pirámide**
José A. Gandia-Blasco
Polyethylene
Fluorescent lamps
H: 181cm (72in)
W: 30cm (12in)
D: 30cm (12in)
Gandia Blasco SA, Spain
www.gandiablasco.com

(right)
**Lamp, Liquid Light
Drop 4 Outdoor**
Hopf + Wortmann,
Büro für Form
Polyethylene,
aluminium
E27, ESL (energy-
saving lamps)
recommended (normal
bulbs: max 100W)
H: 100cm (39in)
Diam: 36cm (14⅛in)
Next, Germany
www.next.de

(left)
**Series of lamps,
Tree 4000**
Pete Sans
Polyethylene
2 x PL-L 120V 36W
(4000-03)
2 x PL-L 120V 24W
(4005-03)
1 x PL-T Triple
4-Pin 120V 18W
(4010-03)
H: 64, 184 or
260cm (25¼,
72½ or 102in)
Vibia Inc, US
www.vibialight.com

(above)
Lamp, Lampion
Emmanuel Gallina
Silicone
1 x E27 30W
fluorescent FBT
or 1 x E27 40W
incandescent IAA/C
H: 27cm (10⅝in)
Diam: 15 cm (5⅞in)
Rotaliana srl, Italy
www.rotaliana.it

(above)
Lights, Lightree
Loetizia Cenzi
Polyethylene
Energy-saving bulb:
1 x E27–15W
H: 45, 100, 150
or 200cm (17¾,
39, 59 or 78in)
W: 30, 64, 95 or
130cm (11¾,
25, 37 or 51in)
Slide srl, Italy
www.slidedesign.it

(right)
Lights, Myflower
Flavio Lucchini
Polyethylene
Energy-saving bulb:
3 x E27–25W
H: 180cm (70in)
W: 120cm (47in)
D: 20cm (7⅞in)
Slide srl, Italy
www.slidedesign.it

(above)
Luminous pouffe,
Campanone Pouff
Paolo Grasselli
Polyethylene
230V connection or
system rechargeable
by means of power
supply or solar panel
H: 42cm (16½in)
Diam: 33cm (13in)
Modo Luce srl, Italy
www.modoluce.com

(above)
Vase, Giò
Monster Light
Giò Colonna Romano
Polyethylene
Light bulb: 1 × E27.
Energy-saving
bulb 105W
H: 92, 133 or 184cm
(36, 52 or 72in)
Diam: 110, 145
or 210cm (43,
57 or 82in)
Slide, Italy
www.gnr8.biz

(left, above, right)
Portable lamp, Grumo
Stéphane Joyeux
Aluminium, PMMA
Energy-saving lamp
(fluocompact light
bulbs or LED)
Diam: 42–72cm
(16½–28in)
Roger Pradier
Lighting, France
www.roger-pradier.com

(facing page)
Lamp, Kanpazar
Jon Santacoloma
Polyethylene
Fluorescent tubes
2 x 55W (2G11) or
2 x 21W (G5)
H: 80 or 150cm
(31 or 59in)
B.Lux, Spain
www.grupoblux.com

(right)
Floor lamp, Bag
Carlo Colombo
Thermo-plastic
expansion
Bulb:
1 x max 60W
E14 round opal
2 x max 100W
E27 opal; dimmer
H: 140cm (55in)
W: 68cm (26in)
D: 31cm (12¼in)
Penta srl, Italy
www.pentalight.it

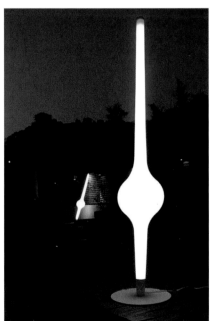

(above)
Lamp, Sticklight
Michael Young
Low-density
polyethylene, steel
1 x 70W T8
fluorescent
H: 196cm (77in)
Diam (at widest point
of the lamp):
30cm (11¾in)
Diam (base):
40cm (15¾in)
Innermost, UK
www.innermost.net

(right)
**Lamp, Havana
Outdoor Terra**
Jozeph Forakis
Polyethylene
1 x 60W incandescent
bulb/1 x 23W
fluorescent bulb
H: 170cm (66in)
Diam: 23cm (9in)
Foscarini srl, Italy
www.foscarini.com

(right)
**Pool lamps,
Waterproof**
Héctor Serrano
Polyethylene
E-10 4.8V 0.75A
H: 53cm (20in)
W: 23cm (9in)
Metalarte SA, Spain
www.metalarte.com

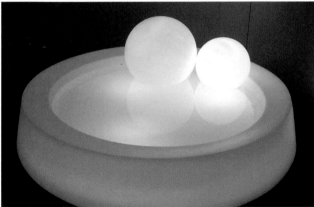

(above and right)
**Light pot, Giò
Piatto Light**
Giò Colonna Romano
Polyethylene
Energy-saving bulb:
1 x E27–25W
H: 48 or 50cm
(18⅞ or 19in)
Diam: 145 or 210cm
(57 or 82in)
Slide srl, Italy
www.slidedesign.it

(left)
**Light table with solar
cell-powered LED
lamp, Ivy**
Paola Navone
Metal
LED
H: 40cm (15¾in)
Diam: 53cm (20in)
Emu Group SpA, Italy
www.emu.it

(left)
**Outdoor parasol,
table and light
system, Po'light**
J. M. Ferrero
Galvanized metal,
waterproof fabric
Internal LED
lighting system
H (parasol):
200cm (78in)
Diam: 180cm (70in)
Puntmobles S.L., Spain
www.puntmobles.es

(above)
Balcony lamp, Sling
Michael Hilgers
Stainless steel,
polycarbonate
E14 energy-saving
bulb
H: 74cm (29in)
Diam: 17cm (6¾in)
Rephorm, Germany
www.rephorm.de

(right)
Lamp, Zola
Uli Guth
Stainless steel,
aluminium
E-14 max 2 x 40W
mate/2-G 13 22W
H: 65 or 100cm
(25 or 39in)
Diam: 29cm
(11⅜in)
Metalarte SA, Spain
www.metalarte.com

(left)
Lamp, Soil Lamp
Marieke Staps
Glass, copper,
zinc, soil, LED
H: 30cm (11¾in)
W: 15cm (5⅞in)
D: 15cm (5⅞in)
Marieke Staps,
the Netherlands
www.mariekestaps.nl

(above)
Lighting, Nanit t 1
Ramón Ubeda,
Otto Canalda
Rotation-moulded
polyethylene
Hal E-27 max 150W
Diam: 40cm (15¾in)
Metalarte SA, Spain
www.metalarte.com

(right)
Floor lamp, Flora
Future Systems
Aluminium,
polyethylene
1 x 24W 2G11
(fluorescent)
H: 208cm (82in)
W: (of the arch):
172cm (68in)
Diam: 43cm
(16⅞in)
FontanaArte SpA, Italy
www.fontanaarte.it

(above)
**Small building,
Sitooterie II**
Thomas Heatherwick
Anodized aluminium,
aluminium tubes glazed
with orange acrylic
H: 240cm (94in)
W: 240cm (94in)
L: 240cm (94in)
Heatherwick Studio, UK
www.heatherwick.com

(left)
**Lighting fixture,
Light House**
Thomas Sandell
White painted metal,
matt acrylic
75W E27 or
18W compact
fluorescent lamps
H: 60cm (23in)
W: 30cm (11¾in)
D: 40cm (15¾in)
Zero, Sweden
www.zero.se

(above)
**Lighting, Urchin
Softlight**
Todd MacAllen,
Stephanie Forsythe
Non-woven
polyethylene textile
(Tyvek©)
5–15W compact
fluorescent / 110-
120V (N. America),
220-240V (Europe)
26.5 x 30cm
(10½ x 11½in)
42 x 43.5cm
(16½ x 17in)
57 x 57cm
(22½ x 22½in)
76 x 76cm (30 x 30in)
molo design, Canada
www.molodesign.com

(left)
Solar outdoor lamp, Zoe Solar
Wolfgang Pichler, Robert Steinböck
Galvanized and powder-coated steel, white acrylic glass
H: 185cm (72in)
Diam: 47cm (18½in)
Viteo Outdoors, Austria
www.viteo.at

(above)
Light, Grande Costanza Open Air
Paolo Rizzatto
Stainless steel, polycarbonate
250W (HSGST E27) or 23W (FBT E27)
H: 230cm (90in)
Diam: 70cm (27in)
Luceplan, Italy
www.luceplan.com

(above)
Lamp, Inout
Ramón Ubeda, Otto Canalda
Polyethylene
E-27 max 60W /E-27 max 2 x 23W
H: 215cm (84in)
Diam: 52cm (20in)
Metalarte SA, Spain
www.metalarte.com

(below)
Lamp, Belvedere Clove
Antonio Citterio
with Toan Nguyen
Bronze
LED
H: 50 or 90cm
(19 or 35in)
Diam: 9cm (3½in)
Flos SpA, Italy
www.flos.com

(right)
Lamp, Lightscape
Jan Jander
Acrylic, aluminium,
white concrete
150W halogen flood or
23W fluorescent flood
H: 122cm (48in)
W: 30cm (12in)
L: 30cm (12in)
Jan Jander Architecture
+ Design LLC, US
www.janjanderad.com

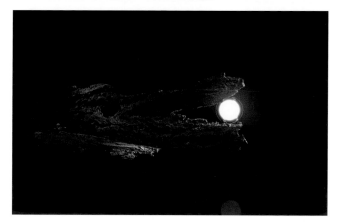

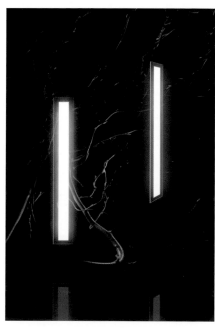

(above and right)
All-in-one lighting system, Lumiblade
Philips Design
Organic LED (OLED)
Philips, the Netherlands
www.philips.com

(above)
**Lighting fixture,
The Great JJ Outdoor**
Centro Stile
Aluminium
1 x max 70W
GX24q-6
H (max extension):
420cm (165in)
L (max extension):
385cm (152in)
Diam: (diffuser):
56.4cm (22in)
I Tre (brand division of
FDV Group SpA), Italy
www.fdvgroup.com

(above)
Lamp, Floor A
Alfredo Chiaramonte,
Marco Marin
Glass fibre
LED
H (max): 200cm (78in)
Diam (base):
60cm (23in)
Emu Group SpA, Italy
www.emu.it

(left)
**Floor light,
SuperArchimoon
Outdoor**
Philippe Starck
Die-cast aluminium,
polycarbonate,
stainless steel
1 x max 230W E27
QT48 HSGS/F
H: 214cm (84in)
W: 242cm (95in)
Flos SpA, Italy
www.flos.com

(above)
**Pendant lamp,
Campanone
Sospenzione**
Paolo Grasselli
Polyethylene
Power cable with
IP 68 connector
Diam: 33 or 51cm
(13 or 20in)
Modo Luce srl, Italy
www.modoluce.com

(left)
Lamp, Lady Mary
Marc Sadler
Polyethylene base
structure with
lacquered and
striped stem
2 fluorescent lamps
2 x 28W
H: 208cm (82in)
Diam (upper):
70cm (27in)
Diam (lower):
53cm (20in)
Serralunga, Italy
www.serralunga.com

(above)
**Outdoor
lamp, Wanda**
Leonhard Palden
Granite, galvanized
and powder-coated
steel
Power LED, works
with battery
H: 212cm (83cm)
W: 29cm (11⅜in)
L: 150cm (59in)
Viteo Outdoors, Austria
www.viteo.at

Jason Bruges

Jason Bruges describes himself as an "architect-turned-artist-stroke-innovator," and is one of a number of creative individuals who challenge the boundaries between art, architecture and interaction design, moving effortlessly between disciplines. His studio, founded in Shoreditch, London, in 2001, has an output that ranges from architectural and art installations to intelligent design and interaction design and events, in projects around the world. He is interested in cities, urban spaces and how people occupy them, using light to describe new spaces and new ideas in dynamic, theatrical ways. A staff that includes qualified architects, set designers, lighting and interaction designers gives you a sense of the studio's extensive output, while an examination of a random selection of projects illustrates the size and scope of the studio's output: a light installation on London Bridge (2008); interior lamps designed with Established & Sons (2009); interactive visuals for George Michael's live show (2006). More recently, the studio, together with Martin Richman, have won London 2012 Olympic Bridges Competition to create visuals, audio, light and tactile elements and installations in the Olympic Park.

Bruges is at the cutting edge of lighting technology and innovation. At the core of his work is a fascination for light, its potential and its effects. "I see light," he says, "as a medium, which is dynamic, malleable, controllable, flexible and works in conjunction with so many other things, interwoven with texture diffusion, materials, sound and other things that modulate at the same time as it does." He continues, "the studio works with dynamic ephemeral, time-based work, a lot of which deals with light, but, there are also other elements which complement light, such as the architectural qualities of things – sound, texture, vibration, but light is the predominant sense at the forefront of Western visual culture, so it crops up

at the forefront of discussion and it crops up a lot in our work."

Bruges originally trained as an architect and worked for Foster & Partners in London and Hong Kong, but his fascination with light and sound led him to work as an interaction designer at Imagination, working on experiential design performance. The domestic garden is not an area in which Bruges specializes; he tends to work on a much larger scale. It is as an innovator that his work has a direct influence on what our gardens will be like in the future.

As you might imagine of someone whose output is so diverse, Bruges' sources of inspiration are as varied as his studio's projects. "I admire someone like Moholy Nagy," he says, "for creating theatrical sets and dynamics with light, and people using structures like Buckminster Fuller." Bruges also cites the American fine artist James Turrell, who uses light to describe extraordinary spaces and the architect Cedric Price, whom Bruges admires for "making space more adaptable and flexible".

Why does Bruges think we are witnessing such an unprecedented interest in exterior lighting. "Lighting," he says, "is an evolving field. People are getting more and more exposure to wonderful lighting design in public spaces in municipal and office buildings and technology is evolving - It's a very primeval thing". And he sees our fascination with outdoors as symptomatic of our "endless human bonding with things that are ephemeral, always changing, always dynamic, whether it's a bonfire, or the wind blowing across the trees, it is that quality which is delightful".

And what does Bruges predict the next big thing will be for gardens? "Organic LEDs, (OLEDs)," he says, "will revolutionize the way people use lighting". Small, energy-efficient OLEDs are made of carbon-based materials and are, therefore, organic, which means they can be built in very fine, thin sheets. The Lumiblade from Philips is just one example of this technology, which is set to

dramatically change the way we manipulate light to enhance architecture, landscaping or objects. Lumiblade has a unique quality, producing constant light of almost any colour, and, unlike traditional LEDs, it can illuminate a wide area evenly. "Another interesting area," Bruges says, "is the use of lasers as a light source".

And will Jason Bruges Studio move on to domestic garden design? "We work with a lot of landscape architects," he says, "and we're sort of toying with the idea of doing Chelsea Flower Show." If Jason Bruges Studio does pursue this idea, you can be sure, that one thing that will definitely be in full bloom is the lighting.

(above)
Miniture LED wind turbine light, Mathmos Wind Light
Jason Bruges
Polypropylene
3 LED Lights
(no electricity, no batteries, just wind)
H: 20cm (7⅞in)
Mathmos Ltd, UK
www.mathmos.com

(left)
Lamp, Light Wind
Judith de Graauw
Polyester, steel
LED lights x 4
H: 240cm (94in)
W: 215cm (84in)
D: 38cm (15in)
Demakersvan,
the Netherlands
www.demakersvan.com

(right)
Oil lamp, Lighthouse
Christian Bjørn
Porcelain,
stainless steel
Lamp oil
H: 24.5, 37.5, 52.5
or 67.5cm (9⅞,
15, 20 or 26in)
Diam: 13.5, 15, 18 or
19cm (5⅜, 5⅞,
7⅛in or 7½in)
Menu A/S, Denmark
www.menu.as

(above)
Torch, Lympos
Flöz Design
Stainless steel, wood
H: 155cm (61in)
Diam: 17cm (6¾in)
Blomus GmbH,
Germany
www.blomus.com

(right)
Torch, Palos
Flöz Design
Stainless steel, wood
H: 151cm (59in)
Diam: 4cm (1⅝in)
Blomus GmbH,
Germany
www.blomus.com

(below and right)
**Solar-powered
LED Lamp for
water bottles,
SOLARBULB™**
MINIWIZ Design Team
ABS/PP Plastic
0.1W High Power LED
Diam: 1cm (⅜in)
MINIWIZ Sustainable
Energy Development
Ltd, Taiwan
www.hymini.com
www.miniwiz.com

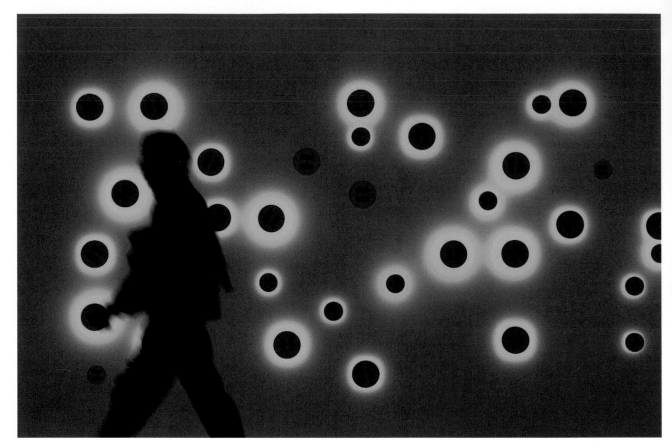

(above)
**Light controlling
device, Kaleidolight**
Kawamura–Ganjavian
(Studio KG)
Glass, aluminium
Defracted natural
daylight
W (handle):
22cm (8⅝in)
W (glass):
14cm (5½in)
L: 68cm (26in)
Solfox Design, Spain
www.solfoxdesign.com
www.studio-kg.com

(above)
Light, Dio
Jonas Kressel,
Ivo Schelle
Aluminium
anodized matt
QPar-CBC
16/50W/230V/GZ
10/cool beam
Diam (light):
14cm (5½in)
IP44 Schmalhorst
GmbH & Co. KG,
Germany
www.ip44.de

(right)
**Floor light,
Tamburo Pole**
Tobia Scarpa
Die-cast aluminium
1 x 57W GX24q-5
TC-T/E FSQ
Diam: 35cm
(13¾in)
Flos SpA, Italy
www.flos.com

(left)
Panel light, Wave®
Verónica Martinez
LG Hi-Macs
LEDs, 220V
H: 300cm (118in)
W: 135cm (53in)
D: 15cm (5⅞in)
Touch By, Spain
www.touchby.com

(above)
Light, Cone
Jonas Kressel,
Ivo Schelle
Stainless steel matt
PAR38/ max 120W/
E27 or LED-W
10 x 2.5W/ LED-RGB
14 x 2.5W
Diam: 14cm (5½in)
IP44 Schmalhorst
GmbH & Co. KG,
Germany
www.ip44.de

(left)
**UV lamp spray can
and glow canvas,
Glow Graffiti**
Random International
The Glow Company
Ltd, UK
www.glow.co.uk

(left)
Lighting fixture, Base
R. Aosta
Die-cast aluminium,
acrylic
18W compact
fluorescent
lamps or LED
H: 10cm (3⅞in)
W: 30cm (11¾in)
D: 10.7cm (4⅜in)
Zero, Sweden
www.zero.se

(above)
Wall lamp, Medito
Marco Mascetti,
MrSmith Studio
Die-cast aluminium
3 x 1W 12V LED
H: 7.5cm (3in)
L: 5.8cm (2¼in)
D: 7.5cm (3in)
FontanaArte SpA, Italy
www.fontanaarte.it

(left)
**Wall-/ceiling-
mounted luminaire,
Nikko+21/VV**
Roberto Fiorato
Aluminium, glass,
stainless steel
1 x max. 13W compact
fluorescent bulb
H: 21.3cm (8¼in)
W: 14.8cm (5⅞in)
D: 13cm (5⅛in)
Prisma – Performance
in Lighting, Italy
www.pil-uk.com

(above)
**Light, Morgan
45° Outside**
Daifuku Design
Aluminium
1 x 9W max (Gx53) or
1 x 1.5W max (Gx53)
LED version
Diam: 9cm (3½in)
L: 16cm (6¼in)
D: 8.7cm (3½in)
Carpyen S.L., Spain
www.carpyen.com

(above)
Lighting fixture, Droppen
Thomas Sandell
Die-cast aluminium, glass
75W E27 or 13/18W compact fluorescent lamps
H: 25cm (9⅞in)
D: 20cm (7⅞in)
Zero, Sweden
www.zero.se

(above)
Wall lamp, Corrubedo
David Chipperfield
Stainless steel, polycarbonate
1 x 27W max E27 (fluorescent)
H: 30cm (11¾in)
L: 21cm (8¼in)
D: 9cm (3½in)
FontanaArte SpA, Italy
www.fontanaarte.it

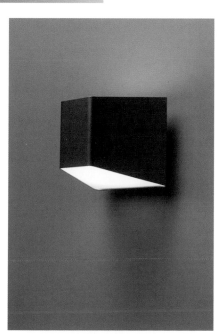

(above)
Lighting fixture, Allright
Per Sundstedt
Anodized aluminium, acrylic
18W compact fluorescent lamps
H: 9cm (3½in)
L: 26cm (10¼in)
Zero, Sweden
www.zero.se

(left)
Lighting fixture, A.01
Kjellander & Sjöberg Arkitektkontor
Anodized aluminium, acrylic
75W E27 or 18W compact fluorescent lamps
H: 19cm (7½in)
W: 18.5cm (7¼in)
D: 23cm (9in)
Zero, Sweden
www.zero.se

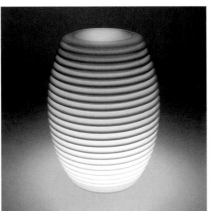

(right)
Lamp, Top Pot Light
Ron Arad
Polyethylene
1 fluorescent lamp
energy saver
20W (E27)
H: 100cm (39in)
Diam: 65cm (25in)
Serralunga, Italy
www.serralunga.com

(above)
Lamp, Vas-One light
Luisa Bocchietto
Polyethylene
1 fluorescent
lamp energy
saver 20W (E27)
H: 120cm (47in)
Diam (upper):
130cm (51in)
Diam (lower):
70cm (27in)
Serralunga, Italy
www.serralunga.com

(left)
**Lamp, New Pot High
Light**
Paolo Rizzatto
Polyethylene
1 fluorescent lamp
energy saver
20W (E27)
H: 90cm (35in)
Diam (upper):
35cm (13¾in)
Diam (lower):
24cm (9½in)
Serralunga, Italy
www.serralunga.com

(above)
**Multipurpose
recreational
stool with light,
Porcino Light**
Aldo Cibic
Polyethylene
1 fluorescent lamp
energy saver
20W (E27)
H: 50cm (19in)
Diam (seat):
35cm (13¾in)
Serralunga, Italy
www.serralunga.com

(above)
**Ceiling light, Romeo
Outdoor C3**
Philippe Starck
Die-cast aluminium,
polycarbonate,
stainless steel
1 x max 150W E27
QT48 HSGS/F
Diam: 55cm (21in)
Flos SpA, Italy
www.flos.com

(above)
Ceiling lamp, Amigo
Gonzalo and
Miguel Milá
Metal, plastic
Fluorescent T16-R
22W/827 2GX13
230V (small)
Fluorescent T16-R
55W/827 2GX13
230 V (medium)
Fluorescent T16-R
2x60W/830 2GX13
230 V (large)
Diam: 31, 41 or 62cm
(12¼ , 16⅛ or 24in)
Santa & Cole, Spain
www.santacole.com

(above)
Light, Light Disc
Alberto Meda,
Paolo Rizzatto
Polycarbonate
55W/40W/22W
(FSC T5, 2GX13)/
32W (FSC T9, G10q)
D: 5.5 or 6.7cm
(2¼ or 2⅝in)
Diam: 32 or 40cm
(12⅝ or 15¾in)
Luceplan, Italy
www.luceplan.com

(above)
**Wall light, Romeo
Outdoor W**
Philippe Starck
Die-cast aluminium,
polycarbonate,
stainless steel
1 x max 100W E27
QT48 HSGS/F
H (lamp): 23cm (9in)
Diam: 34cm
(13⅜in)
Flos SpA, Italy
www.flos.com

(right)
**Lamp, Belvedere
Round**
Antonio Citterio,
Toan Nguyen
Bronze
LED
H: 50 or 84cm
(19 or 33in)
Diam: 35cm
(13¾in)
Flos SpA, Italy
www.flos.com

(left)
**Recessed wall
luminaire, Cubis Q**
Karsten Winkles
Cast aluminium
TC-D 18 Watt
H: 19.4cm (7⅝in)
W: 19.4cm (7⅝in)
Hess AG, Germany
www.hess.eu

(above)
Lighting, Edge
IP44
Stainless steel
T5 39W
L: 100cm (39in)
W: 11.5cm (4½in)
D: 6cm (2⅜in)
Sabz, France
www.sabz.fr

(right)
**Illuminating
strip, Ledia**
Karsten Winkels
Stainless steel,
tempered safety
glass strip
LED
L: 24, 46, 69 or 91cm
(9½, 18⅛,
27 or 35in)
Hess AG, Germany
www.hess.eu

(left)
**Walk-over
inground luminaire,
Waylight Prisma**
Performance in Lighting
Aluminium, glass,
stainless steel
LEDs
Various dimensions
Prisma – Performance
in Lighting, Italy
www.pil-uk.com

(above)
**Architectural
lighting, Dolma
80 Outdoor**
Kristof Pycke
Aluminium,
galvanized steel
QR-CBC51/
HIT-TC or LED
H (max):
600cm (236in)
W: 8cm (3⅛in)
D: 12.5cm (4⅞in)
Kreon, Belgium
www.kreon.com

(left)
**Lighting system,
Naster**
Emanuela Pulvirenti
Stainless steel,
tempered glass,
aluminium
Single T5 electronic
fluorescent lamp
24/39/54W or LEDs
L: 123, 94 or 65cm
(48, 37 or 25in)
Castaldi Illuminazione,
Italy
www.
castaldilluminazione.com

(facing page)
Lamps, Nawa
Antoni Arola
Extruded aluminium
2 G–11 max 36W
H: 80, 125 or 250cm
(31, 49 or 98in)
Metalarte SA, Spain
www.metalarte.com

(left)
Lighting, Glim Cube
Piero Castiglioni
Polymethacrylate,
Zama 15, stainless
steel, polypropylene
LED
H: 35cm (13¾in)
iGuzzini, Italy
www.iguzzini.com

(above)
Light, Empty
J. Ll. Xuclà
Aluminium, wood
Fluorescent
TC-F 36W 2G10
H: 45cm (17¾in)
W: 45cm (17¾in)
L: 45cm (17¾in)
Dab, Spain
www.dab.es

(left)
**Floor light, Garden
Soft**
Metis lighting
Stainless steel
1 x 3W LED
H: 30cm (11¾in)
FontanaArte SpA, Italy
www.fontanaarte.it

(above)
Lighting, Euclide
Studio Arnaboldi
Aluminium, stainless
steel, polycarbonate,
glass
Metal halide or
halogen lamps
H: 100cm (39in)
W: 19.4cm (7⅝in)
D: 19.4cm (7⅝in)
iGuzzini, Italy
www.iguzzini.com

(left)
Lamp, 45 Adj FL 1
Tim Derhaag
Anodized
aluminium, teak
1 x 24W 2G11 FSD
H: 44cm (17⅜in)
L: 20cm (7⅞in)
Flos SpA, Italy
www.flos.com

(above)
**Candle holder,
Portavelas**
José A. Gandia-Blasco
Anodized aluminium
H: 150cm (59in)
W: 10cm (3⅞in)
D: 10cm (3⅞in)
Gandia Blasco SA, Spain
www.gandiablasco.com

(left)
Adjustable light, 45
Tim Derhaag
Die-cast aluminium
1 x 24W 2G11 FSD
H: 20cm (7⅞in)
L: 44cm (17⅜in)
Flos SpA, Italy
www.flos.com

(right)
Lighting pole, 17°
Lighting Pole
Francisco Providência
Stainless steel
1 x 150W tinned
iodides light bulb
H: 453cm (178in)
Diam: 11.4cm
(4½in)
Larus, Portugal
www.larus.pt

(right)
Floor light,
Chilone Terra
Ernesto Gismondi
Brushed steel
5W LED
H: 45, 90 or 180cm
(17¾, 35 or 70in)
W: 6cm (2⅜in)
D: 14cm (5½in)
Artemide SpA, Italy
www.artemide.com

(left)
Floor light,
Ciclope Terra
Alessandro Pedretti,
Studio Rota & Partner
Die-cast aluminium,
extruded aluminium
10W LED
H: 50 or 90cm
(19 or 35in)
W: 15cm (5⅞in)
D: 5cm (2in)
Artemide SpA, Italy
www.artemide.com

(left)
Lamp, Nagy
Joan Verdugo
Transparent, injected
polycarbonate,
extruded aluminium
2G11 18W
H: 32.5cm (13in)
H (poles): 60,
100 or 150cm
(23, 39 or 59in)
W: 13.5cm (5⅜in)
L: 18.8cm (7½in)
Marset, Spain
www.marset.com

(left)
**Lighting fixture,
W-Bell**
Wingårdhs Arkitekter
Painted steel, acrylic,
aluminium
42W compact
fluorescent lamp,
metal halide or
high-pressure sodium
H: 45.6cm (18⅛in)
Diam: 52cm (20in)
Zero, Sweden
www.zero.se

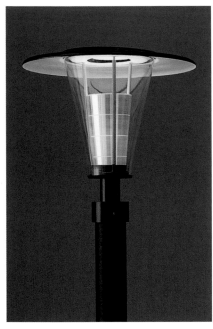

(above)
**Lighting fixture,
Berzeli**
Per Sundstedt
Painted aluminium,
acrylic
57W compact
fluorescent lamp,
metal halide or
high-pressure sodium
H: 56cm (22in)
Diam: 60cm (23in)
Zero, Sweden
www.zero.se

(above)
Light column, Vigo
Jean-Marc Schneider
Aluminium, PMMA
1xRX7S, HIT-DE-CE
70W
H: 250cm (98in)
Diam: 16cm (6¼in)
Hess AG, Germany
www.hess.eu

(right)
Lighting fixture, Rib
Niklas Ödmann
Painted steel, teak
Compact
fluorescent lamp
H: 57cm (22in)
Diam: 30cm
(11¾in)
Zero, Sweden
www.zero.se

(left)
**Flexible post lamp,
LP Hint**
Helena Tatjana Eliason
Aluminium, acrylic,
polycarbonate
42W TC–TEL HF,
57W TC–TEL or
70W HIE/HIT
H: 300cm (118in)
Diam: 47.7cm
(18⅞in)
Louis Poulsen
Lighting, Sweden
www.louispoulsen.com

(right)
Light, Lumicono
Trislot
Stainless steel
3 x 3W power LED
(one colour or RGB)
H: 82.4cm (32in)
Diam: 10.9cm
(4⅜in)
Trislot, Belgium
www.trislot-deco.com

Furniture

(above)
Bench, Bench with Backrest/Home Collection
Wolfgang Pichler
Stainless steel, teak
H: 82cm (32in)
W: 53cm (20in)
L: 180cm (70in)
Viteo Outdoors, Austria
www.viteo.at

(above)
Bench with armrest, La Superfine
Thesevenhints
Laminate, steel, polyurethane
H: 77cm (30in)
W: 103cm (41in)
D: 72cm (28in)
Miramondo GmbH, Austria
www.miramondo.com

(left)
Bench, Bench 62/ Home Collection
Wolfgang Pichler
Stainless steel, teak
H: 47cm (18½in)
W: 62cm (24in)
L: 190 cm (74in)
Viteo Outdoors, Austria
www.viteo.at

(left)
**Garden bench,
Bench**
Tom Lovegrove
Water-jet cut steel,
steel tube, oak,
powder coating
H: 70cm (27in)
D: 45cm (17¾in)
L: 120cm (47in)
Tom Lovegrove, UK
www.rocketgallery.com
www.tomlovegrove.com

(above)
Bench, Giulietta
Paolo Rizzatto
Polyethylene
H: 100cm (39in)
H (seat):
45cm (17¾in)
W: 67cm (26in)
L: 185cm (72in)
Serralunga, Italy
www.serralunga.com

(left)
Bench, Romeo
Paolo Rizzatto
Polyethylene
H: 96cm (37in)
H (seat):
46cm (18⅛in)
W: 61cm (24in)
L: 115cm (45in)
Serralunga, Italy
www.serralunga.com

(above)
**Modular seating
system, Ghisa**
Riccardo Blumer
Matteo Borghi
Cast iron
H: 72cm (28in)
D: 62cm (24in)
Alias, Italy
www.aliasdesign.it

(right)
**Outdoor seating,
Come Rain Or Shine**
Robert Richardson
Recycled plastic
H: 80cm (31in)
W: 185cm (72in)
D: 61cm (24in)
Robert Richardson
Design, UK
www.robrichdesign.co.uk

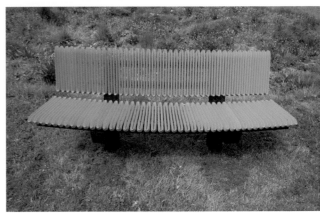

(right)
**Bench with two
integrated flower
pots, Romeo
& Juliet**
Koen Baeyens, Stijn
Goethals, Basile Graux
Jatoba wood, polyester
H: 48cm (18⅞in)
W: 73.5cm (29in)
L: 320cm (126in)
Extremis, Belgium
www.extremis.be

(left)
Bench, Peddy
Mindscape
Grass, metal
H: 37.5cm (15in)
W: 165cm (65in)
D: 90cm (35in)
Mindscape
Corporation, Japan
www.mindscape.jp

(above)
Steel bench, Origami
Harald Guggenbichler
Steel
H: 45cm (17⅞in)
L: 154cm (60⅝in)
Fermob, France
www.fermob.com

(right)
Bench, Serpentine
Dean and Jason Harvey
FSC-certified hardwood
with granite, stainless steel
H: 48cm (18⅞in)
W: 46cm (18in)
L: 230cm (90½in)
Factory Furniture, UK
www.factoryfurniture.co.uk

(right)
Bench, Wings Bench
Pinar Yar, Tugrul Gövsa
Composites,
polyurethane
foam, teak
H: 75cm (29in)
W: 216cm (85in)
D: 31cm (12¼in)
Govsa Composites,
Turkey
www.gaeaforms.com

(above)
Bench, Step Bench
Pinar Yar, Tugrul Gövsa
Composites,
polyurethane foam
H: 55cm (21in)
W: 120cm (47in)
D: 53 (20in)
Govsa Composites,
Turkey
www.gaeaforms.com

(left)
Bench, Monolith
Wim Segers
Teak with Sikaflex®
H: 66cm (26in)
L: 270cm (106¼in)
D: 56.5cm (22¼in)
Tribù, Belgium
www.henryhalldesigns.com

(left)
Bench/table,
Into the Woods
Susan Bradley
Powder-coated
stainless steel
H: 40cm (15¾in)
W: 40cm (15¾in)
L: 125cm (49in)
Susan Bradley
Design, UK
www.susanbradley.co.uk

(above)
Bench/Open storage
seat, Double Hollow
Lars Dahmann
Polyethylene fibre,
aluminium
H: 45cm (17¾in)
L: 90cm (35in)
D: 45cm (17¾in)
Lebello, US
www.lebello.com

(left)
Bench, Sushi Outdoor
Bartoli Design
Anodized aluminium
H: 75cm (29in)
W: 41cm (16⅛in)
L: 180cm (70in)
Kristalia, Italy
www.kristalia.it

(right)
Informal bench for indoor/outdoor use, Loop
Christophe Pillet
Polyethylene
H: 40cm (15¾in)
W: 50 (19in)
L: 180cm (70in)
Serralunga, Italy
www.serralunga.com

(facing page)
Bench, Bdlove Bench
Ross Lovegrove
Rotation-moulded polythene
H: 94cm (37in)
W: 265cm (104in)
D: 129cm (51in)
Bd Barcelona, Spain
www.bdbarcelona.com

(above)
Seating, Shell Bench
Richard Mackness
Glass-reinforced concrete
H: 80cm (31in)
W: 60cm (23in)
L: 180cm (70in)
Urbis Design, UK
www.urbisdesign.co.uk

(right)
Bench, E-turn
Brodie Neill
Lacquered fibreglass
H: 42cm (16½in)
W: 56cm (22in)
l ; 185cm (72in)
Kundalini Srl, Italy
www.kundalini.it

(left)
Bench, Coral Bench
Chris Kabatsi
Powder-coated,
laser-cut steel
H: 46cm (18in)
W: 44cm (17½in)
L: 152cm (60in)
Arktura, US
www.arktura.com

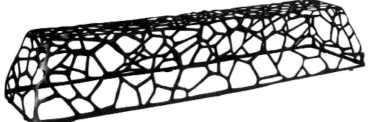

(above)
Bench, Cell Bench
Anon Pairot
Sand-cast aluminum
H: 37cm (14½in)
W: 52cm (20½in)
L: 198cm (78in)
Restrogen, Thailand
www.fordandching.com

(above)
**Seating, Bed
of Roses**
Design Studio
Muurbloem
Coated foam
H: 45cm (17¾in)
W: 300cm (118in)
Feek, Belgium
www.feek.be

(left)
Bench, Petit Jardin
Tord Boontje
Steel, powder coating
H: 125cm (49in)
W: 125cm (49in)
L: 218cm (86in)
Studio Tord Boontje,
France
www.tordboontje.com

(above)
**Seating, Bloc/
Cementum Collection**
Gerd Rosenauer
Concrete
H: 32cm (12⅝in)
W: 58cm (22in)
L: 116cm (46in)
Viteo Outdoors, Austria
www.viteo.at

(above)
Seating, Flor®
Mansilla & Tuñón
Cast stone
H: 42cm (16½in)
Escofet, Spain
www.escofet.com

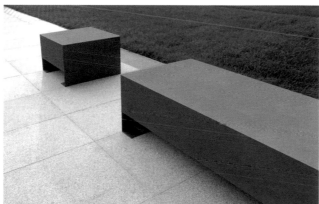

(left)
Bench, Leichtgewicht
Thesevenhints
Steel plates,
highly condensed
fibre concrete
H: 40cm (15¾in)
L: 60 or 180cm
(23in or 70in)
D: 60cm (23in)
Miramondo public
design GmhH, Austria
www.miramondo.com

(left)
Bench, Trapecio
Antonio Montes,
Montse Periel
Solid larch wood
H: 57cm (22in)
H (seat): 40cm
(15¾in)
W: 540cm (212in)
D: 81cm (31in)
Santa & Cole, Spain
www.santacole.com

(above)
**Lounge model,
Avenue First Block**
Alex Bergman
Polyester with
PVC coating,
polystyrene foam
H: 47cm (18½in)
W: 58cm (22in)
D: 58cm (22in)
Fatboy, the
Netherlands
www.fatboy.com

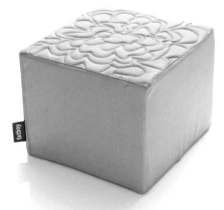

(left)
**Lounge model,
Avenue First Parc**
Alex Bergman
Polyester with
PVC coating,
polystyrene foam
H: 47cm (18½in)
W: 58.5cm (23in)
D: 58.5cm (23in)
Fatboy, the
Netherlands
www.fatboy.com

(above)
**Modular seating
system, Univers
Collection**
Wolf Udo Wagner
Fm-foam soft
H (one module):
up to 63cm (24in)
W (one module):
up to 85cm (33in)
D (one module):
up to 85cm (33in)
Fischer Möbel GmbH,
Germany
www.fischer-moebel.de

(right)
**Pouffe, Club
Ottoman 01**
Studio Arne Quinze
Q&M foam™
H: 37cm (14⅝in)
W: 60cm (23in)
L: 75cm (29in)
Quinze & Milan, Belgium
www.quinzeandmilan.tv

(left)
Pouffe, Club Pouf 01
Studio Arne Quinze
Q&M foam
H: 37cm (14⅝in)
L: 75cm (29in)
Quinze & Milan, Belgium
www.quinzeandmilan.tv

(right)
**Cushions and seating,
Neo Livingstones**
Stéphanie Marin
Neoprene, silicon
fibres, polyurethane
Smallest cushion:
28 x 17 x 15cm
(11 x 6¾ x 5⅞in)
Largest cushion:
100 x 64 x 35cm
(39 x 25 x 13¾in)
Smallest seating:
70 x 60 x 40cm
(27 x 23 x 15¾in)
Largest seating:
200 x 140 x 70cm
(78 x 55 x 27in)
Smarin, France
www.smarin.net

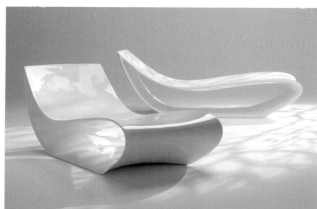

(left)
Chaise longue, Sign
P. Cazzaniga
Polyamide
H: 62cm (24in)
W: 69cm (27in)
L: 178cm (70in)
MDF Italia, Italy
www.mdfitalia.com

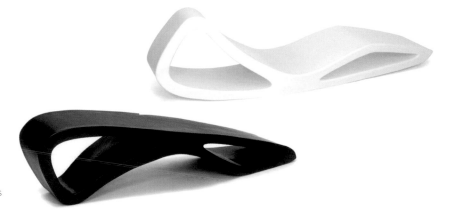

(right)
**Reversible seating,
B'kini Chair**
Wiel Arets
Polyethylene
H: 60cm (23in)
W: 60cm (23in)
L: 200cm (78in)
Gutzz, the Netherlands
www.gutzz.com

(right)
**Chaise longue,
Sunset 6-630 C**
Clemens Hüls
Aluminium, weave
of Raucord
synthetic fibres
H: 36–49cm
(14⅛–19¼in)
W: 80cm (31in)
L: 220cm (86in)
Rausch Classics
GmbH, Germany
www.rausch-classics.de

(above)
**Chaise longue, Chill/
The 35 Collection**
Frog Design
Rotation-moulded
polyethylene
H: 84cm (33in)
W: 71cm (28in)
L: 157cm (62in)
Landscapeforms, US
www.landscapeforms.com

(left)
**Sun lounger, Tandem
Sun Lounger**
Thomas Sauvage
Aluminium,
Batyline®, teak
H: 37cm (14⅝in)
W: 90cm (35in)
D: 209cm (82in)
Ego Paris, France
www.egoparis.com

(left)
Sun lounger, Zoe
Moredesign
di Morello Alessandro
Polyethylene
H: 35cm (13¾in)
L: 240cm (94in)
D: 69cm (27in)
Myyour, Italy
www.myyour.eu

(right)
Sun lounger, Cloe
Moredesign
di Morello Alessandro
Polyethylene
H: 59cm (23in)
L: 220cm (86in)
D: 63cm (24in)
Myyour, Italy
www.myyour.eu

(left)
**Ergonomic sunbed,
Pascià**
Ciro Matino
Aluminium
H: 40cm (15¾in)
W: 82cm (32in)
L: 200cm (78in)
Giallosole by
Mix srl, Italy
www.giallosole.eu

(above)
Sunbed, RIVA
Schweiger & Viererbl
HPL synthetic
material, steel
H: 24cm (9½in)
W: 70cm (27in)
L: 210cm (82in)
Conmoto, Germany
www.conmoto.com

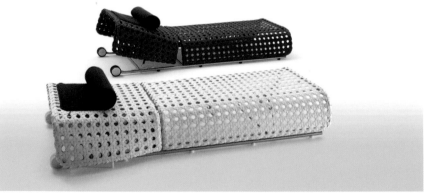

(above)
**Lounger, Canasta
Chaise Longue**
Patricia Urquiola
Aluminium,
polyethylene,
stainless steel
H: 36cm (14⅛in)
W: 101cm (40in)
L: 200cm (78in)
B&B Italia SpA, Italy
www.bebitalia.com

(right)
**Sunbed, Striped
Lettino**
Ronan and Erwan
Bouroullec
Steel tube
H: 32cm (12⅝in)
W: 68.5cm (27in)
L: 203cm (80in)
Magis SpA, Italy
www.magisdesign.com

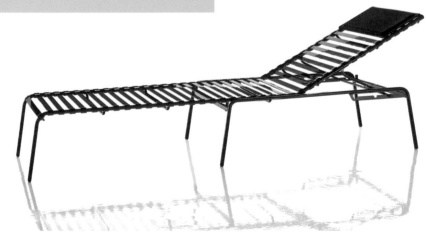

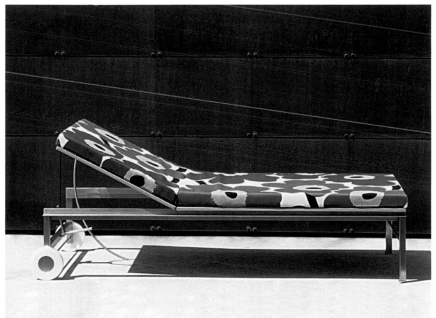

(above)
Lounge chair, Costa Lounge Chair
Erwin Vahlenkamp, Geert Van Acker
Powder-coated steel, corded (synthetic) leather weaving
H: 80cm (31in)
W: 60cm (23in)
L: 180cm (70in)
EGO² BV, the Netherlands
www.ego2.com

(above)
Sunbed, Day-bed Pontile
Jacques Toussaint
Stainless steel, marine plywood, cotton Unikko Marimekko® mattress
H: 39cm (15⅜in)
L: 190cm (74in)
D: 75cm (29in)
Dimensione Disegno srl, Italy
www.dimensionedisegno.it

(left)
Sunbed, Sunny Longer
Tord Boontje
Tubular steel
H: 75cm (29in)
L: 200cm (78in)
D: 70cm (27in)
Moroso SpA, Italy
www.moroso.it

(above)
Chaise longue, Frame
Francesco Rota
Aluminium profiles
upholstered with rope
or Aquatech braids
H: 70cm (27in)
H (seat): 31cm
(12¼in)
W: 74cm (29in)
L: 157cm (62in)
Paola Lenti srl, Italy
www.paolalenti.com

(above)
**Chaise longue,
Cortiça**
Daniel Michalik
Recycled cork
H: 64cm (25in)
W: 50cm (19in)
L: 183 (72in)
DMFD, US
www.danielmichalik.com

(right)
**Chaise longue,
Striped Chaise
Longue**
Ronan and Erwan
Bouroullec
Steel tube
H: 85cm (33in)
W: 68cm (26in)
L: 149.5cm (59in)
Magis SpA, Italy
www.magisdesign.com

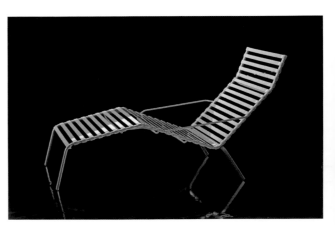

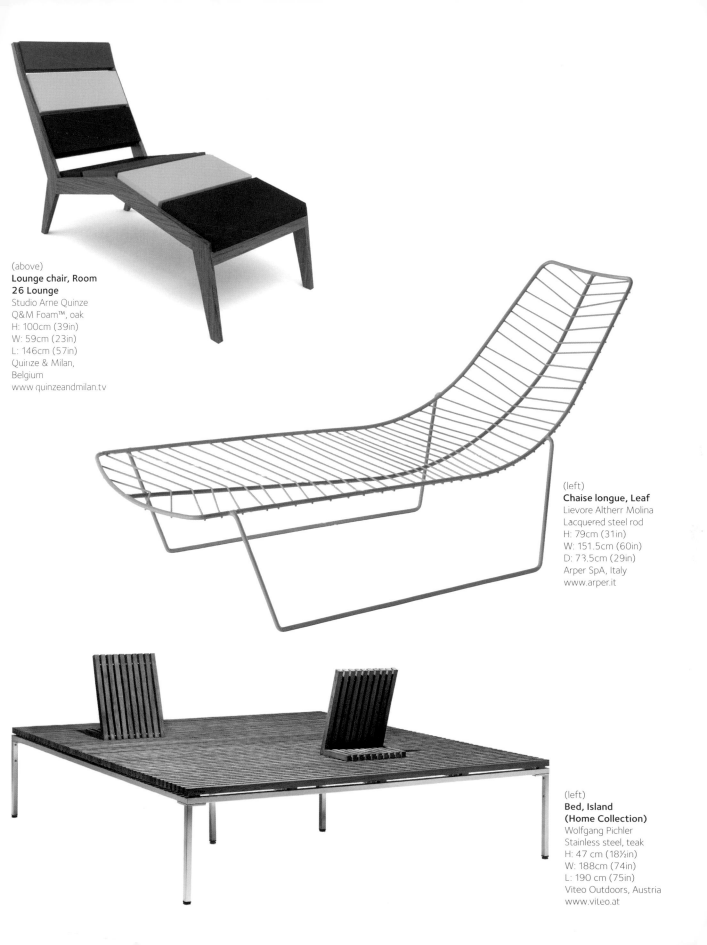

(above)
Lounge chair, Room 26 Lounge
Studio Arne Quinze
Q&M Foam™, oak
H: 100cm (39in)
W: 59cm (23in)
L: 146cm (57in)
Quinze & Milan, Belgium
www.quinzeandmilan.tv

(left)
Chaise longue, Leaf
Lievore Altherr Molina
Lacquered steel rod
H: 79cm (31in)
W: 151.5cm (60in)
D: 73.5cm (29in)
Arper SpA, Italy
www.arper.it

(left)
Bed, Island (Home Collection)
Wolfgang Pichler
Stainless steel, teak
H: 47 cm (18½in)
W: 188cm (74in)
L: 190 cm (75in)
Viteo Outdoors, Austria
www.viteo.at

(left)
**Rotational chair,
XP Chair**
Alex Milton
Recycled polyurethane
H: 66cm (26in)
W: 50cm (19in)
L: 74.5cm (29in)
Outgang, UK
www.outgang.com

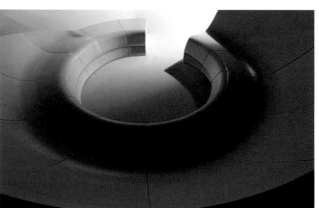

(above)
Seating, Atollo
p.èn.lab
DuPont™ Corian®
H: 90cm (35in)
W: 300cm (118in)
L: 340cm (133in)
Escho, Italy
www.escho.it

(above)
Chair, Xxl
Kettal Studio
Kettal Puur
polyurethane
foam, aluminium
H: 46cm (18⅛in)
W: 36cm (14⅛in)
D: 38cm (15in)
Kettal, Spain
www.kettal.es

(right)
Sofa, MT2
Ron Arad
Rotational-moulding
polyethylene
H: 85cm (33in)
H (seat): 42cm
(16½in)
W: 180cm (70in)
D: 85.4cm (33in)
Driade, Italy
www.driade.com

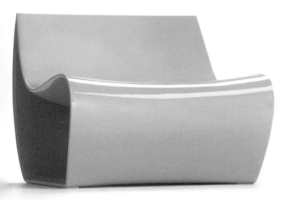

(above)
Armchair, Sign
Piergiorgio Cazzaniga
Lacquered polyamide
H: 62cm (24in)
H (seat): 38cm (15in)
L: 74cm (29in)
D: 76cm (30in)
MDF Italia, Italy
www.mdfitalia.it

(above)
Chair, Disk
Karim Rashid
Fibreglass
H: 75cm (29in)
W: 112cm (44in)
D: 108cm (43in)
Ferlea, Italy
www.ferlea.com

(left)
Chair, Vintage Chaise
Bram Bollen
Polypropylene,
electro-polished
stainless steel
H: 85cm (33½in)
W: 80cm (31½in)
L: 117cm (46in)
Tribù, Belgium
www.henryhalldesigns.com

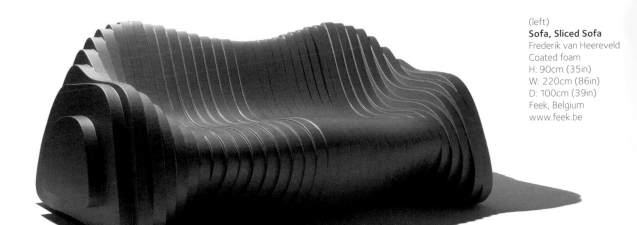

(left)
Sofa, Sliced Sofa
Frederik van Heereveld
Coated foam
H: 90cm (35in)
W: 220cm (86in)
D: 100cm (39in)
Feek, Belgium
www.feek.be

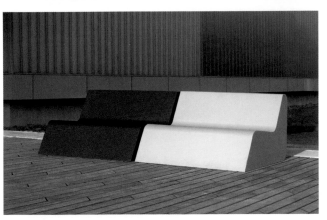

(left)
Sofa, Dalilips
Salvador Dalí with
Oscar Tusquets Blanca
Medium-density,
rotational-moulded
polyethylene
H: 73cm (28in)
H (seat): 37cm
(14⅜in)
W: 170cm (66in)
D: 100cm (39in)
Bd Barcelona, Spain
www.bdbarcelona.com

(above)
**Modular seating
system, Ellipses**
Giuseppe Viganò
Lacquered steel
H: 64cm (25in)
H (seat): 25cm
(9⅞in)
D: 90cm (35in)
Bonacina Pierantonio
srl, Italy
www.
bonacinapierantonio.it

(right)
**Sofa, Orca
Square Set**
Frederik van Heereveld
Coated foam
H: 65cm (25in)
W: 112cm (44in)
D: 112cm (44in)
Feek, Belgium
www.feek.be

(left)
Seating, Sonntag
Tim Kerp
Powder-coated
steel, birch plywood,
felt or foam
H: 76cm (29in)
L: 120cm (47in)
Tim Kerp Design
Development,
Germany
www.tim-kerp.de

(above)
Sofa, BendyBay
Danny Venlet
Polyester,
stainless steel
H: 61cm (24in)
H (seat): 39cm
(15⅜in)
D: 98cm (38in)
Viteo Outdoors, Austria
www.viteo.at

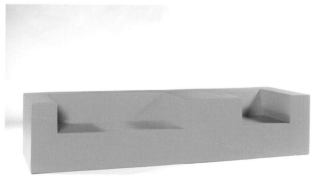

(left)
Sofa, Club
Studio Arne Quinze
Q&M foam™
H: 69cm (27in)
L: 307cm (121in)
Quinze & Milan,
Belgium
www.quinzeandmilan.tv

(above)
**Outdoor waterbed,
Lylo**
Danny Venlet
Polyester
H: 35cm (13¾in)
Diam: 220cm (86in)
Viteo Outdoors, Austria
www.viteo.at

(facing page)
Seating, Osorom
Konstantin Grcic
Fibreglass, resin,
multi-layered techno-
polymer composite
H: 35cm (13¾in)
Diam: 120cm (47in)
Moroso SpA, Italy
www.moroso.it

(above)
**Table seating
combination, DoNuts**
Dirk Wynants
Rubber tyre, ballistic
nylon, polyester
H: 75cm (29in)
H (seating): 45cm
(17¾in)
Diam: 190cm (74in)
Extremis, Belgium
www.extremis.be

(right)
Sofa, Flow
Dennis Marquart
Gel-coated fibreglass
H: 74cm (29in)
L: 240cm (94in)
D: 110cm (43in)
Nola, Sweden
www.nola.se

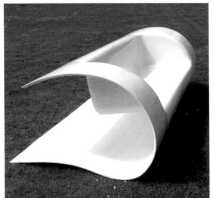

(right)
**Modular and
luminous bar,
Jumbo Corner**
Jorge Nàjera
Polyethylene
Energy-saving bulb:
2 x E27-25W
H: 110cm (43in)
W: 80cm (31in)
D: 80cm (31in)
Slide srl, Italy
www.slidedesign.it

(above)
**Modular furniture
system, Manhattan**
Kettal Studio
Kettal Puur
Polyurethane foam,
aluminium
H: 60cm (23in)
H (seat): 25cm
(9⅞in)
D: 92cm (36in)
Kettal, Spain
www.kettal.es

(right)
**Beanbag, Fatboy®
Original**
Alex Bergman
Polyester with
PVC coating
W: 140cm (55in)
L: 180cm (70in)
Fatboy, the
Netherlands
www.fatboy.com

(left)
**Modular sofa system,
Friends Collection**
Robin Delaere
Aluminium, PE fibre
H: 75cm (29in)
W (each piece):
85cm (33in)
Some, Belgium
www.some.be

(above)
Three-seat sofa, Bel Air
Sacha Lakic
Aluminium,
polyethylene resin,
Twitchell fabric
and cushions in
Missoni Home
H: 62cm (24in)
L: 150cm (59in)
D: 100cm (39in)
Roche Bobois, France
www.roche-bobois.com

(above)
Sofa, Hoop
Arik Levy
Steel, fabric
H: 66cm (26in)
W: 160, 200 or 240cm
(63, 78 or 94in)
D: 100cm (39in)
Living Divani srl, Italy
www.livingdivani.it

(above)
Modular sofa, One
Marc Sadler
Polyethylene, fabric
H: 69cm (27in)
H (seat): 38cm (15in)
L (single element):
120cm (47in)
L (double element
with one arm):
255cm (100in)
D: 100cm (39in)
Serralunga, Italy
www.serralunga.com

(right)
Pouffe, Island
Luisa Bocchietto
Polyethylene, metal
H: 36cm (14⅛in)
W: 130cm (51in)
L: 130cm (51in)
Serralunga, Italy
www.serralunga.com

(above)
**Gazebo with benches
and table, Pine Valley**
Talocci Design
Stainless steel
H: 213cm (84in)
W: 202cm (80in)
L: 202cm (80in)
Foppapedretti SpA,
Italy
www.foppapedretti.it

(above)
**Turntable room,
Capsule Room**
Mark
Suensilpong
Teak, stainless
steel, fabric
H: 220cm (87in)
W: 256cm (101in)
D: 180cm (71in)
Jane Hamley Wells, US
www.janehamleywells.com

(right)
**Lounge island,
Kosmos**
Dirk Wynants
Solimbra, synthetic
leather, outdoor fabric,
indoor leather, etc.
H (couch):
76cm (29in)
Diam: 260cm (102in)
Extremis, Belgium
www.extremis.be

(left and below)
Collection of modular furniture, Atmosphere
Marcel Wanders
Kettal Puur foam, fabric, aluminium, fibreglass
H (central and corner module): 60cm (23in)
W (central and corner module): 95cm (37in)
D (central and corner module): 95cm (37in)
Kettal, Spain
www.kettal.es

(above)
Lounge bed, Maui Bed
Rowena Tse
Aluminium, UV-protected synthetic-weave, water-resistant cushions
H: 200cm (79in)
H (seat): 42cm (16½in)
W: 180cm (70in)
D: 120cm (47in)
Zuo Modern, US
www.zuomod.com

(right)
Gazebo, Oasis 026 Gazebo
Rodolfo Dordoni
Teak, painted iron, white polyester fabric
H: 240cm (94in)
W: 272cm (107in)
L: 272cm (107in)
Roda srl, Italy
www.rodaonline.com

(right)
**Day bed/Swing bed,
Swing Bed**
Garpa
High-quality synthetic
fibre, satin-finished
stainless steel,
upholstery
H: 190cm (74in)
W: 260cm (102in)
D: 134cm (53in)
Garpa Garden & Park
Furniture Ltd, Germany
www.garpa.de

(above)
**Garden swing,
Nao-Nao**
Yolanda Herraiz
Anodized aluminium,
yacht fabric
H: 200cm (78in)
H (seat): 45cm
(17¾in)
W: 215cm (84in)
L: 254cm (100in)
Gandia Blasco SA, Spain
www.gandiablasco.com

(below)
**Rocking chair,
Thinking Machine**
Eduardo Baroni
Steel, polyurethane
H: 200cm (78in)
W: 254cm (100in)
L: 215cm (84in)
Sintesi, Italy
www.gruppo-sintesi.com

(right)
Hammock, Wave
Erik Nyberg,
Gustav Ström
Electro-polished
stainless steel,
perforated fabric
H: 370cm (146in)
W: 250cm (98in)
L: 290cm (114in)
Royal Botania, Belgium
www.royalbotania.com

(above)
Hammock, E–Z
Bo Larsen,
Zaki Molgaard
Inox, Batyline®
H: 62cm (24in)
W: 57cm (22in)
L: 230cm (90in)
Royal Botania, Belgium
www.royalbotania.com

(right)
**Hammock, Leaf
Hammock**
Pinar Yar, Tugrul Govsa
Composites, sailing
rope, Dacron
H: 20cm (7⅞in)
W: 150cm (59in)
L: 260cm (102in)
GAEAforms, Turkey
www.gaeaforms.com

(left)
Armchair, Pop
Enzo Berti
Polyurethane foam
H: 75cm (29in)
W: 90cm (35in)
Ferlea, Italy
www.ferlea.com

(below)
**Monobloc sofa,
Tokyo-pop**
Tokujin Yoshioka
Polyethylene
H: 75.5cm (29in)
H (seat): 42cm
(16½in)
W: 177cm (70in)
D: 78cm (30in)
Driade, Italy
www.driade.com

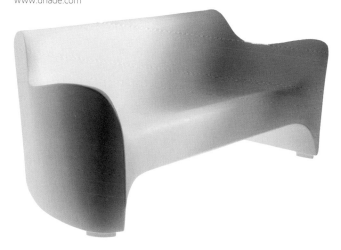

(above)
**Armchair for indoor
and outdoor use,
Moor(e)**
Philippe Starck
Lacquered nylon
H: 91cm (35in)
H (seat): 45.8cm
(18⅛in)
W: 129.5cm (51in)
D: 101cm (39in)
Driade SpA, Italy
www.driade.com

(left)
**Beach chair,
LEAF XXL**
Frank Ligthart
Hand-woven Dedon
fibre, powder-coated
aluminium
H: 42cm (16½in)
W: 151cm (59in)
L: 254cm (100in)
Dedon, Germany
www.dedon.de

(above)
Armchair, Ivy
Paola Navone
Metal
H: 66cm (26in)
L: 110cm (43in)
D: 90cm (35in)
Emu Group SpA, Italy
www.emu.it

(above)
Sofa, Q-Couch
Frederik van Heereveld
Expanded
polypropylene
12 x 89 x 80cm
(4¾ x 35 x 31½in)
Feek, Belgium
www.feek.be

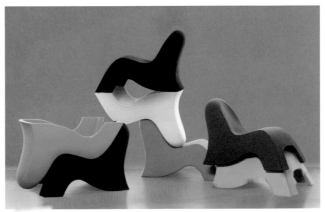

(left)
Seat, I'm Dreaming
Dominic Symons
Rotation-moulded
polyethylene
H: 72cm (28in)
H (seat): 34cm (13¾in)
W: 00cm (33in)
D: 97cm (38in)
Maxdesign, Italy
www.maxdesign.it

(above)
Chair and table, Sponeck
Julia von Sponeck
Fibre cement
H (chair):
60cm (23in)
H (table):
25cm (9⅞in)
W: 50cm (19in)
L (chair):
77.5cm (30in)
L (table): 50cm (19in)
Eternit AG, Switzerland
www.eternit.ch

(above)
Armchair, O-Nest
Tord Boontje
Rotation-moulded
polyethylene
H (seat):
42cm (16½in)
H: 77cm (30in)
W: 66cm (26in)
D: 69cm (27in)
Moroso SpA, Italy
www.moroso.it

(left)
Seating, Chubby and Chubby Low
Marcel Wanders Studio
Polyethylene
H (Chubby):
56cm (22in)
H (Chubby Low):
30cm (11¾in)
W (Chubby):
120cm (47in)
W (Chubby Low):
75cm (29in)
L (Chubby):
130cm (51in)
L (Chubby Low):
85cm (33in)
Slide srl, Italy
www.slidedesign.it

(right)
Sofa, Cima
Raneo Lounge
Hendrik Steenbakkers
Stainless steel, Batyline
H: 70.5cm (28in)
W: 200cm (78in)
D: 78cm (30in)
FueraDentro, the
Netherlands
www.fueradentro.com

(above)
Lounge chair, Cool Chair
Charlie Davidson
Welded, punched
steel sheet and
powder coating
H: 75cm (29in)
W: 98cm (38in)
D: 100cm (39in)
Charlie Davidson
Studio, Sweden
www.charlie-davidson.com

(right)
Lounge chair, Kyoto
Lounge Chair
Wolf Udo Wagner
Fm-foam soft
H: 75cm (29in)
W: 73cm (28in)
D: 95cm (37in)
Fischer Möbel GmbH,
Germany
www.fischer-moebel.de

(above)
**Lounge chair,
Hee Lounge Chair**
Hee Welling
Electro-plated solid
steel, powder coating
H: 67cm (26in)
H (seat): 38cm (15in)
W: 72cm (28in)
Hay, Denmark
www.hay.dk

(above)
Lounge chair, Leaf
Lievore Altherr Molina
Lacquered steel rod
H: 73cm (28in)
W: 85cm (33in)
D: 64.5cm (25in)
Arper SpA, Italy
www.arper.it

(above)
Armchair, Tropicalia
Patricia Urquiola
Stainless steel,
woven cord
H (seat): 37cm
(14⅝in)
H: 78cm (30in)
W: 94cm (37in)
D: 87cm (34in)
Moroso SpA, Italy
www.moroso.it

(below)
**Low chair, Striped
Poltroncina**
Ronan and Erwan
Bouroullec
Steel tube
H: 68.5cm (27in)
H (seat): 36cm
(14⅛in)
W: 66.5cm (26in)
D: 76.5cm (30in)
Magis SpA, Italy
www.magisdesign.it

(above)
**Table/sofa/lounge
chair, Zero Collection**
Enzo Calabrese,
Fabio Meliota
Lacquered steel
H (table): 66cm (26in)
H (sofa and lounge
chair): 70cm (27in)
W (sofa):
137cm (54in)
W (lounge chair):
78cm (30in)
Diam (table):
120cm (47in)
L'abbate srl, Italy
www.lacollection.it

(above)
**Small monobloc
armchair, Clover**
Ron Arad
Polyethylene
H: 75.5cm (29in)
H (seat): 42.5cm
(16⅞in)
W: 66cm (26in)
D: 54cm (21in)
Driade, Italy
www.driade.com

(above)
Lounge chair, Brasilia
Ross Lovegrove
Polyurethane
H: 83cm (32in)
H (seat): 39cm
(15⅜in)
W: 58cm (22in)
L: 100cm (39in)
Zanotta SpA, Italy
www.zanotta.it

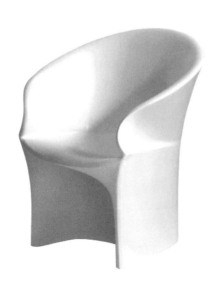

(right)
Armchair, Mermaid
Tokujin Yoshioka
Polyethylene
H: 83.5cm (33in)
H (seat): 43.5cm
(17⅜in)
W: 70cm (27in)
D: 65cm (25in)
Driade, Italy
www.driade.com

(right)
**Hooded armchair,
Outdoor Showtime**
Jaime Hayon
Rotation-moulded,
medium-density
polyethylene
H: 168cm (66in)
H (seat): 43cm
(16⅞in)
W: 90cm (35in)
D: 82cm (32in)
Bd Barcelona, Spain
www.bdbarcelona.com

(above)
Armchair, Shadowy
Tord Boontje
Tubular steel
H (seat): 31cm
(12¼in)
H: 140cm (55in)
W: 98cm (38in)
D: 82cm (32in)
Moroso SpA, Italy
www.moroso.it

(right)
**Outdoor seating,
Armchair, Sofa and
Poltronas Showtime
Outdoor**
Jaime Hayon
Rotation-moulded,
medium-density
polyethylene
Various dimensions
Bd Barcelona, Spain
www.bdbarcelona.com

(left)
Armchair, Kloe
Marco Acerbis
Rotation-moulded
polyethylene
H: 68cm (26in)
H (seat): 38cm (15in)
L: 75cm (29in)
D: 80cm (31in)
Desalto, Italy
www.desalto.it

(right)
**Furniture collection,
Bent**
Christophe De La
Fontaine, Stefan Diez
Laser-cut, bent
aluminium
H (table): 42cm
(16½in)
H (armchair):
69cm (27in)
W (table): 49cm
(19¼in)
W (armchair):
93cm (36in)
Moroso SpA, Italy
www.moroso.it

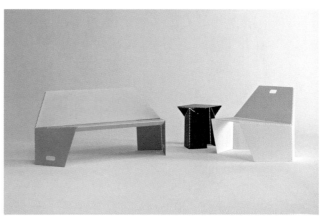

(left)
Ottoman, MB 5
Mario Bellini
Polyethylene
H: 36cm (14⅛in)
W: 56cm (22in)
D: 56cm (22in)
Heller Inc, US
www.helleronline.com

(left)
**Lounge chair,
IZ Collection**
Francesc Rifé
Lacquered aluminium
H: 69cm (27in)
W: 71.5cm (28in)
D: 64.5cm (25in)
Samoa, Spain
www.samoadesign.com

(above)
Chair, 06
Maarten Van Severen
Stainless steel, integral
skin polyurethane
foam, integrated
leaf springs
H: 73.2cm (28in)
W: 49.5cm (19in)
D: 73cm (28in)
Vitra, Switzerland
www.vitra.com

(left)
Armchair, Wavy
Ron Arad
Stainless steel,
polyethylene
H: 98cm (38in)
W: 68cm (27in)
D: 66cm (26in)
Moroso SpA, Italy
www.moroso.it

(right)
**Parasol base/table/
stool, Cube**
Jan Melis
Polyethylene
H: 45cm (17¾in)
W: 45cm (17¾in)
D: 45cm (17¾in)
Sywawa, Belgium
www.sywawa.be

(above)
**Four stools and
central table/stool,
Schtum**
Scene
Polyurethane-coated
foam
H: 45cm (17¾in)
W (packed together):
100cm (39in)
L (packed together):
100cm (39in)
Feek, Belgium
www.feek.be

(right)
**Coffee table/
Ottoman, InOut
41/43**
Paola Navone
Ceramic
H: 37cm (14⅝in)
W: 40cm (15¾in)
D: 40cm (15¾in)
Gervasoni SpA, Italy
www.gervasoni1882.it

(right)
Chair, Treccia
Enrico Franzolini
Metal, polypropylene
H: 76.5cm (30in)
W: 55cm (21in)
D: 52.5cm (20in)
Accademia, Italy
www.accademiaitaly.com

(above)
Chair, Baba
Gunilla Hedlund
Zinc-plated,
powder-coated steel
H: 82cm (32in)
H (seat): 45cm
(17¾in)
W: 50cm (19in)
D: 47cm (18½in)
Nola Industrier, Sweden
www.nola.se

(left)
**Seating,
Conversation Chair**
Ana Linares
Powder-coated steel
H: 60cm (23in)
W: 60cm (23in)
L: 90cm (35in)
Ana Linares Design, US
www.analinaresdesign.com

(left)
**Folding chair,
Clip Chair**
Blasius Osko,
Oliver Deichmann
Solid beech
H: 71.5cm (28in)
H (seat): 30cm
(11¾in)
W: 85cm (33in)
D: 65cm (25in)
Moooi, the Netherlands
www.moooi.com

(left)
**Chair, Forest
Garden Chair**
Robby and Francesca
Cantarutti
Aluminium
H: 83cm (32⅝in)
H (seat): 44cm
(17⅜in)
W: 43cm (17in)
D: 45cm (17¾in)
Fast Italy, Italy
www.gomodern.co.uk

(right)
**Cantilever chair,
Myto**
Konstantin Grcic
BASF Ultradur®
High Speed plastic
H: 82cm (32in)
H (seat): 46cm
(18⅛in)
W: 51cm (20in)
D: 55cm (21in)
Plank, Italy
www.plank.it

(left)
Chair, Net
Sam Johnson
Powder-coated
steel wire
H: 80cm (31½in)
W: 58.3cm (23in)
D: 58.3cm (23in)
Mark, UK
www.markproduct.com

(left)
Chair, Chair_One
Konstantin Grcic
Aluminium
H: 82cm (32in)
W: 55cm (21in)
D: 59cm (23in)
Magis SpA, Italy
www.magisdesign.com

(above)
Chair, Vegetal
Ronan & Erwan
Bouroullec
Polyamide
H: 81.3cm (32in)
H (seat): 46cm
(18⅛in)
W: 60.6cm (24in)
D: 57.7cm (22in)
Vitra AG, Switzerland
www.vitra.com

(right)
Chair, Bauhaus
Robby Cantarutti
Plastic, steel
H: 80cm (31½in)
W: 53cm (20in)
D: 56cm (22in)
Figurae di JDS, Italy
www.jds.eu

(below)
Easy chair, Soft Egg
Philippe Starck
Polypropylene
H: 74cm (29in)
H (seat): 43.5cm
(17⅜in)
W: 60.5cm (24in)
D: 57.5cm (22in)
Driade, Italy
www.driade.com

(above)
**High easy chair,
Out/In**
Philippe Starck with
Eugeni Quitllet
Polyethylene,
anodized aluminium
H: 147cm (58in)
H (seat): 44cm
(17⅜in)
W: 78cm (31in)
D: 77cm (30in)
Driade, Italy
www.driade.com

(right)
Chair, Go
Ross Lovegrove
Magnesium,
polycarbonate
H: 89.9cm (35⅜in)
H (seat): 46cm
(18⅛in)
W: 49.5cm (19½in)
D: 62.2cm (24½in)
Danerka A/S, Denmark
www.danerka.dk

(above)
Chair, Brillant
Robby and Francesca
Cantarutti
Polycarbonate, metal
H: 80.5cm (31in)
W: 60.5cm (24in)
D: 59cm (23in)
Figurae di JDS, Italy
www.jds.eu

(below)
Chair, Scoop
Denis Santachiara
Brushed stainless steel
tubing, variable-density
multi-layer, composite
techno-polymer
H: 87cm (34in)
W: 55cm (21in)
D: 65cm (25in)
Steelmobil (Industrieifi
Group), Italy
www.steelmobil.com/
www.ifi.it

(left)
Easy chair, Toy
Philippe Starck
Polypropylene
H: 78cm (30in)
H (seat): 43cm
(16⅞in)
W: 61.5cm (24in)
D: 57.5cm (22in)
Driade, Italy
www.driade.com

(above)
**Chair and stool,
Pebble**
Benjamin Hubert
Polyethylene,
solid oak, steel
H (chair): 84cm (33in)
H (stool):
47cm (18½in)
W (chair):
46cm (18⅛in)
W (stool):
40cm (15¾in)
De Vorm, the
Netherlands
www.devorm.nl

(left)
Stool, Bun Bun
Paiwate Wangbon
Resin mosaic
H: 42cm (16½in)
Diam: 57cm (22in)
UO Contract, US
www.uocontract.com

(above)
**Table and shaped
armchairs unit,
Community Set**
Moredesign
Polyethylene
H: 72cm (28in)
Diam: 79cm (31in)
Myyour, Italy
www.myyour.eu

(above)
Stool, Q Stool
Danny Venlet
Outdoor Skai,
stainless steel
H: 47cm (18½in)
Diam: 43cm (16⅞in)
Viteo Outdoors, Austria
www.viteo.at

(left)
Pouffe, BUX
Studio Tweelink
Imitation leather,
foam, polyethylene
H: 55cm (21in)
Diam: 41cm (16⅛in)
Dutch Summer,
the Netherlands
www.dutchsummer.com

(above)
Lounge chair and table set, Obelisk
Frank Ligthart
Hand-woven Dedon fibre, powder-coated aluminium
H (in total): 244cm (96in)
Diam: 80cm (31in)
Dedon, Germany
www.dedon.de

(left)
Chair, Sundance
Stefan Heiliger
Rotation-moulded polyethylene
H: 73cm (28in)
H (seat): 41cm (16⅛in)
W: 61cm (24in)
D: 61cm (24in)
Tonon SpA, Italy
www.tononitalia.com

(above)
Tables, Tölt
Michael Young
Corian, Robinia wood
H (round table):
73cm (28in)
Diam (round table):
75cm (29in)
H (short table):
43.5cm (17⅜in)
W (short table):
41.4cm (16⅛in)
L (short table):
77cm (30in)
Extremis, Belgium
www.extremis.eu

(above)
**Bench/low table,
Quadrant**
David Scott
Certified renewable
cellulose fibre and
resin* (generic
description for material
known under the brand
name Richlite)
H: 38cm (15in)
Diam: 147cm (58in)
Desu Design, US
www.desudesign.com

(right)
Side table, Trip
Pinar Yar, Tugrul Govsa
Composites,
polyurethane
H: 36cm (14⅛in)
W: 62cm (24in)
L: 62cm (24in)
Gaeaforms, Turkey
www.gaeaforms.com

Dirk Wynants

The Belgian company Extremis was at the vanguard of the renaissance of interest in outdoor furniture that took place in the early 1990s. Founder, director and lead designer Dirk Wynants is a larger-than-life character and Extremis designs are a direct reflection of his lifestyle and personality. Wynants also works closely with other international designers such as Michael Young and Arnold Merckx. The term 'Tools for Togetherness', which Extremis has coined, succinctly describes the ethos of the company's products, a range designed for group gatherings and activities from eating to lounging – and with witty titles such as DollyPop, YeeHaa! and DoNots, you sense that these products have been designed for the good times.

There may be humour in the work, but the designs themselves are refreshingly unconventional, and perfectly capture the zeitgeist. "We wanted to design things that brought people together," says Wynants, a desire perfectly illustrated in BeHive (2006), a capacious, circular, upholstered outdoor lounger, (large enough for a dozen or so revellers), with the springy bounce of a trampoline to add to the experience and a canopy to protect from the elements. Then there's the dual function IceCube, a substantial party drinks cooler with integrated lighting. Wynants' latest 'Tool for Togetherness' was commissioned by the Design Museum in Ghent to improve the relationship between audience and speaker but it is a departure from Wynants' usual repertoire: Kosmos Oris is a portable pulpit.

Born in 1964, Wynants is the son of a cabinet-maker. He studied interior and furniture design at the Sint-Lucas School of Architecture in Ghent. He founded Extremis in 1994 – as he says, "I always wanted to start my own business by the time I was 30. So I looked around and thought, what can I offer to the market that's not already there? And I decided it was going to be outdoor furniture as I couldn't find what I wanted as there wasn't a market at that time."

There have been considerable changes in our attitudes to outdoor design since the company began, as Wynants explains. "Traditionally outdoors was not part of the living space. You had all these separate areas in your home where you did certain things. Nowadays the bathroom's become a spa, the kitchen's been integrated with the sitting room and it's become a residential bistro, while outdoors has become a living component in its own right, as important as any of the main rooms in the home".

Wynants has his own theories about why outdoor space is so important now and feels we need to compensate for the rapid march of technology and its effect on us. As he says, "Our lives have changed drastically in the last decade or so, and the pressure on us has changed drastically. I think people are looking for compensation for that. Communication is immediate now – mobile phones, the internet. Today, if you don't have an answer in five minutes everyone gets nervous. We no longer have contact with the seasons;

temperature and lighting in our offices and homes is controlled; we live in great comfort. The most successful travel companies these days are those offering the no-comfort, adventure-style holidays; they compensate for the changes we've had in the last 10–15 years."

Extremis sell work in over 40 countries so Wynants must have observed that different countries have different requirements and tastes. "Of course," he replies, "the further south, the softer the materials become, and the colour of materials change too, cooler and more durable in the north, and more colourful as you travel south."

Unlike some design practices, Extremis does not have a recognizable signature, this is because of the way Wynants approaches the design process. As he explains, "I don't try to find inspiration from other stuff because otherwise there's a risk you'll start designing existing designs, so I try to find inspiration in other things, mostly travel and people. I start by observing how people interact socially – the idea is driven by the function required. I try to recreate the atmosphere of a product." BeHive, for example, was partly inspired by the Bedouin tents of north Africa. "A lot of designers," he says, "work the other way. They start with a certain form or a certain material. I never want to design something in a certain material, I always want to design functional things, to express the design that I have in my mind – to make furniture to bring people together."

(above)
Table and umbrella, Arthur/InUmbra
Dirk Wynants
Table: High-pressure laminate
Umbrella: stainless steel, Airtex® fabric
H (table): 74cm (29in)
Diam (table):
160, 200 or 240cm
(63, 78 or 94in)
Extremis, Belgium
www.extremis.be

(above)
Side table, Helix
Wolfgang C. R. Mezger
Stainless steel
Diam: 56cm (22in)
Fischer Möbel GmbH,
Germany
www.fischer-moebel.de

(above)
Tables, T–Table
Patricia Urquiola
PMMA
H: 28, 36 or 44cm
(11, 14⅛ or 17⅜in)
Diam: 50cm (19in)
Kartell SpA, Italy
www.kartell.it

(above)
Table, Air–Table
Jasper Morrison
Polypropylene
H: 69.5cm (27in)
W: 65cm (25in)
D: 65cm (25in)
Magis SpA, Italy
www.magisdesign.com

(right)
Table, Miura
Konstantin Grcic
Steel
Diam: 60cm (23in)
Plank, Italy
www.plank.it

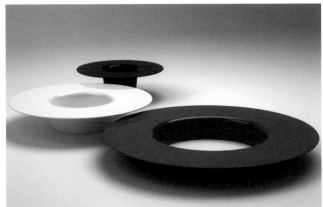

(left)
**Collection of
occasional tables,
Boom**
Todd Bracher
Polyurethane resin
with lacquered finish
H: 32.5, 26 or 20cm
(13, 10¼ or 7⅞in)
Diam: 95, 135 or
175cm)
Serralunga, Italy
www.serralunga.com

(above)
**Table and bench,
Sanmarco**
Gae Aulenti
Steel, laminate
H (table): 73cm (28in)
H (bench): 45cm
(17¾in)
W (table): 80cm (31in)
W (bench): 30cm
(11¾in)
Zanotta SpΛ, Italy
www.zanotta.it

(right)
**Table, Table 90
Home Collection**
Wolfgang Pichler
Stainless steel, laminate
H: 76cm (29in)
W: 90cm (35in)
L: 90cm (35in)
Viteo Outdoors, Austria
www.viteo.at

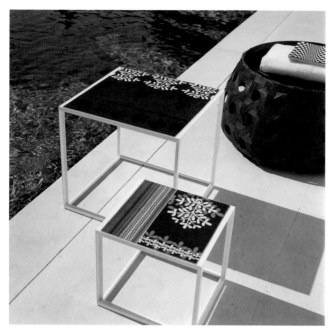

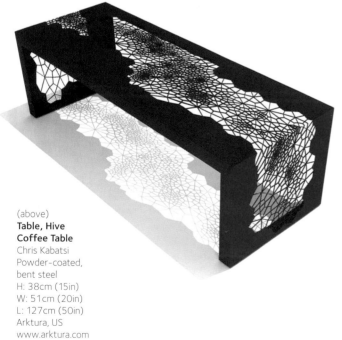

(left)
**Tables, Canasta
Tables**
Patricia Urquiola
Ceramic, steel
H: 31 or 45cm
(12¼ or 17¾in)
W: 33cm or 47cm
(13 or 18½in)
D: 30.5cm or 45cm
(12¼ or 17¾in)
B&B Italia, Italy
www.bebitalia.com

(above)
**Table and bench
collection, Sis**
Vicent Martínez
Aluminium and keraon
by TAU (material with
ceramic origin)
H (table): 75cm (29in)
H (bench):
44cm (17⅜in)
W (table):
206cm (81in)
W (bench):
183cm (72in)
D (table): 90cm (35in)
D (bench): 40cm
(15¾in)
Puntmobles, Spain
www.puntmobles.es

(above)
**Table, Hive
Coffee Table**
Chris Kabatsi
Powder-coated,
bent steel
H: 38cm (15in)
W: 51cm (20in)
L: 127cm (50in)
Arktura, US
www.arktura.com

(left)
**Dining table,
Case Study 6-ft
Stainless Dining
Table Modernica**
Stainless steel, marble
H: 41cm (16in)
W: 183cm (72in)
D: 97cm (38in)
Modernica, California
www.modernica.net

(above)
**Table, High Bar/
Home Collection**
Wolfgang Pichler
Stainless steel, laminate
H: 110cm (43in)
W: 69cm (27in)
L: 190cm (74in)
Viteo Outdoors, Austria
www.viteo.at

(above)
**Table,
La Grande Table**
Xavier Lust
Aluminium
H: 73cm (28in)
W: 80 or 90cm
(31 or 35in)
L (min): 200cm (78in)
L (max): 440cm
(173in)
MDF Italia, Italy
www.mdfitalia.it

(above)
Table, Keramik
Bruno Fattorini
Aluminium, laminated
ceramic
H: 75cm (29in)
W: 97cm (38in)
L: 220cm (86in)
MDF Italia, Italy
www.mdfitalia.it

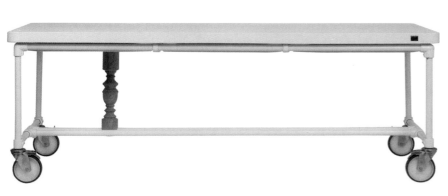

(left)
**Table, Saloon
ral 9010**
Rein Noels
Steel, wood,
coated foam
H: 78cm (30in)
L: 218cm (86in)
D: 88cm (34in)
Sterk-Design,
the Netherlands
www.sterk-design.nl

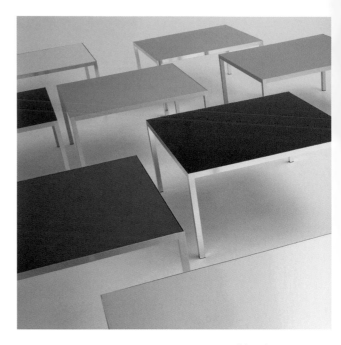

(above)
Coffee tables, LIM04
Bruno Fattorini
Aluminium frame
H: 30cm (11¾in)
MDF Italia, Italy
www.mdfitalia.it

(above)
**Table, Shell
Dining 200**
Jan des Bouvrie
Stainless steel, glass
H: 75cm (29in)
W: 200cm (/8in)
D: 100cm (39in)
FueraDentro, the
Netherlands
www.fueradentro.com

(right)
**Table and
benches, RIVA**
Schweiger & Vierebl
Scratch-resistant HPL
H (table): 72cm (28in)
H (bench):
44cm (17⅜in)
D (table): 70cm (27in)
D (bench):
35cm (13¾in)
L (table): 160,
180 or 220cm
63, 70⅞ or 86⅝in)
L (bench): 156,
176 or 216cm
(61⅜, 69⅜ or 85in)
Conmoto, Germany
www.conmoto.com

(left)
Table, Clothy's
Gerard der Kinderen
Coated foam, steel
H: 75cm (29in)
W: 70cm (27in)
L: 70cm (27in)
Feek, Belgium
www.feek.be

(above)
**Table, VITEO Island
(Home Collection)**
Wolfgang Pichler
Stainless steel, teak
H: 47cm (18½in)
W: 188cm (74in)
L: 188cm (74in)
Viteo Outdoors, Austria
www.viteo.at

(below)
**Table with
four chairs,
Watershed Outdoor
Furniture Set**
Paul Galli
FSC-certified young
teak, stainless steel
H (chair): 83cm
(32½in)
H (table): 76cm (30in)
W (chair): 41cm (16in)
W (table): 99cm (39in)
D (chair): 52cm
(20½in)
D (table):
152cm (60in)
Pirwi, Mexico
www.pirwi.com

(right)
Stackable stool,
Dedal
emiliana design studio
Polyurethane foam,
rotation-moulded
polyethylene
H: 55.1cm (21in)
Diam: 43.5cm
(17⅛in)
Puntmobles, Spain
www.puntmobles.es

(above)
Stool, Sway
Thelermont Hupton
Polyethylene,
polyurethane
H: 34, 50 or 66.5cm
(13⅜, 19 or 26in)
Diam: 21cm (8¼in)
Thelermont Hupton, UK
www.thelermonthupton.com

(above)
Seating, Tumbly
Annet Neugebauer
Polyethylene
H: 48cm (18⅞in)
W: 33cm (13in)
D: 46cm (18⅛in)
De Vorm, the
Netherlands
www.devorm.nl

(right)
Stool, Tokyo-pop
Tokujin Yoshioka
Polyethylene
H: 70cm (27in)
W: 36.5cm (14⅜in)
D: 40cm (15¾in)
Driade, Italy
www.driade.com

(facing page)
Stool, Flod
Azúa-Moliné
Polyethylene
H: 77cm (30in)
W: 41.5cm (16½in)
Mobles 114
Barcelona, Spain
www.mobles114.com

(above)
Stool, Shitake
Marcel Wanders
Rotation-moulded
polyethylene
H: 43cm (16⅞in)
W: 52cm (20in)
D: 37cm (14⅜in)
Moroso SpA, Italy
www.moroso.it

(above)
**Stools, The Fool
on the Hill**
Luca Nichetto
Ceramics
H: 25 or 55cm
(9⅞ or 21in)
W: 45 or 68cm
(17¾ or 37in)
D: 56 or 94cm
(22 or 37in)
Moroso SpA, Italy
www.moroso.it

(right)
Stool, Nook
Patrick Frey
VarioLine®, plastic,
aluminium
W: 42cm (16½in)
D: 42cm (16½in)
Vial GmbH, Germany
www.vial.eu

(left)
Stool, Miura
Konstantin Grcic
Reinforced
polypropylene
H: 81cm (31in)
W: 47cm (18½in)
D: 40cm (15¾in)
Plank, Italy
www.plank.it

(right)
Chair, Waves
Jens Ring Bursche
Polypropylene
H: 80cm (31in)
W: 48.5cm (19¼in)
D: 48cm (18⅞in)
Figurae di JDS, Italy
www.jds.eu

(left)
Coffee table, Tod
Todd Bracher
Polyethylene
H: 52cm (20in)
W: 55cm (21in)
D: 43cm (16⅞in)
Zanotta SpA, Italy
www.zanotta.it

(right)
Stool, Porcino
Aldo Cibic
Polyethylene
H: 50cm (19in)
Diam: 35cm
(13¾in)
Serralunga, Italy
www.serralunga.com

(above)
Potting bench,
Beethoven
Michael Koenig
Aluminium
H: 118cm (46in)
W: 59cm (23in)
L: 110cm (43in)
Flora Wilh. Förster
GmbH & Co. KG,
Germany
www.flora-online.de

(above)
Tree pot and
seating, Treepot
Design Studio Mango
Polyethylene
H: 55cm (21in)
Diam: 150cm (59in)
Gutzz, the Netherlands
www.gutzz.com

(right)
Alternative garden
furniture, The bok.
pitchforkseat
Sander Bokkinga
Wood, steel and rope
H: 70cm (27in)
W: 40cm (15¾in)
D: 5cm (2in)
bok. Sander Bokkinga,
the Netherlands
www.sanderbokkinga.nl

(left)
Shelf, Bibliothek HP9
Hans Hansen
HPL
H: 103cm (41in)
W: 103cm (41in)
D: 29cm (11⅜in)
Hans Hansen h+h
furniture GmbH,
Germany
www.hanshansen.de

(above)
Clothes drier, Alberto
Fabrica
Polyethylene
H: 181cm (71in)
W: 8cm (3⅛in)
L: 96.5cm (38in)
Casamania by
Frezza, Italy
www.casamania.it

(above)
Shelf, Natsiq Outdoor
Frank Lefebvre
Wood, stainless steel
H: 200cam (78in)
L: 230cm (90in)
D: 73cm (28in)
Bleu Nature, France
www.bleunature.com

(right)
Washing line, Saguaro
Davy Grosemans
Rotation-moulded
plastic, aluminium
H: 216cm (85in)
W: 64cm (25in)
D: 10cm (3⅞in)
das ding, Belgium
www.dasding.be

Shelter

(right)
**Outdoor building,
Shack at Hinkle Farm**
Jeffery Broadhurst
Wood, aluminium,
glass, canvas
Building size, including
the deck: 26m² (280ft²)
Jeffery Broadhurst, US
www.broadhurst
architects.com

(above)
**Prefabricated and
flat-pack delivered
house concept,
Mini House –
A Contemporary
Swedish Cottage**
Jonas Wagell
Plywood with phenol
resin film, Styrofoam,
galvanized steel,
aluminium, glass,
impregnated timber
H: 300cm (118in)
W: 425cm (167in)
D (house): 350cm
(138in)
D (pergola room):
350cm (138in)
Mini House/Jonas
Wagell, Sweden
www.minihouse.se

(right)
**Garden pavilion,
EcoCube™ II**
Ecospace
Western red cedar
H: 245cm (96in)
W: 330cm (130in)
D: 330cm (130in)
Ecospace, UK
www.ecospacestudios.com

(above)
Cabin, Read-nest
Dorte Mandrup
Arkitekter
Natural oiled wood
slats, plywood
H: 315cm (124in)
H (skylight):
345cm (136in)
W: 315cm (124in)
L: 315cm (124in)
Dorte Mandrup
Arkitekter, Denmark
www.dortemandrup.dk

(above)
Prefab unit, Rincon 5
Marmol Radziner
Prefab (Leo Marmol,
Ron Radziner)
Steel frame modules,
glass, concrete
tile flooring
61m² (660ft²)
Marmol Radziner
Prefab, US
www.marmolradzinerprefab.com

(right)
**Studio/office/garden
room/flexible space,
The Buckingham**
Green Retreats
Glass, wood
W: 410cm (161in)
L: 516cm (203in)
Green Retreats, UK
www.greenretreats.co.uk

(above)
**Sustainable
micro-building,
big dwelle.ing**
Richard Frankland
Timber frame
structure with various
cladding materials
W: 350cm (138in)
L: 670cm (264in)
dwelle., UK
www.dwelle.co.uk

(above)
**Compact
second home,
Sommarnöjen KS2**
Kjellander+Sjöberg
Arkitektkontor/
Sommarnöjen
Wood
H: 300cm (118in)
W: 385cm (152in)
D: 385cm (152in)
Sommarnöjen, Sweden
www.sommarnojen.se

(facing page)
**Studio, Ecospace
Mono-pitch Studio**
Ecospace
Structually insulated
panel systems
(SIPS), cedar, Bauder
Thermoplan
H: 280cm (110in)
W: 640cm (252in)
D: 380cm (149in)
Ecospace, UK
www.ecospacestudios.
com

(right)
**Sustainable
micro-building
(home office),
office dwelle.ing**
Richard Frankland
Timber frame
structure with various
cladding materials
W: 230cm (90in)
L: 360cm (141in)
dwelle., UK
www.dwelle.co.uk

(above)
**Portable dwelling,
Carré d'Etoiles**
Carré d'Etoiles
Wood, fibreglass,
plexiglass
H: 300cm (118in)
W: 300cm (118in)
D: 300cm (118in)
Carré d'Etoiles, France
www.carre-detoiles.com

(left)
**Retreat,
Summer House**
Todd Saunders,
Tommie Wilhelmsen
Wood
H: 300cm (118in)
L: 410cm (161in)
Saunders Architecture,
Norway
www.saunders.no

(above)
**Multi-purpose
garden project,
Walden**
Nils Holger Moormann
Larch
H: 386cm (152in)
W: 110cm (43in)
L: 650cm (256in)
Nils Holger Moormann
GmbH, Germany
www.moormann.de

(right)
**Modular home
(mini home), Solo**
Andy Thompson,
Sustain Design
Studio Ltd
Red FunderMax
rainscreen cladding
W: 244cm (96in)
L: 1097cm (432in)
Sustain Design Studio
Ltd, Canada
www.sustain.ca

(left and below)
Shelter, Habitable Polyhedron
Architect: Manuel Villa
Carpenter Luis Carlos
Wood structure, wood walls, window metal frame, concrete foundations, metal supports, shingle tiles, acrylic dome
H: 300cm (118in)
W: 300cm (118in)
D: 300cm (118in)
Manuel Villa Arquitecto
www.manuelvillaarq.com

(above and right)
Artificial mobile hedge, Porta Hedge
Justin Shull
Exterior: recycled artificial Christmas trees, trailer, solar electric panels, surveillance cameras
Interior: live plants, field guides, birdsong audio, chalkboards, peep holes, monitors, portable toilet
H: 244cm (96in)
W: 244cm (96in)
L: 640cm (252in)
www.justinshull.us

(above)
**Treehouse, Between
Alder and Oak**
Baumraum
Oak, high-grade steel
W (lower terrace):
250cm (98in)
L (lower terrace):
700cm (275in)
W (cabin):
200cm (78in)
L (cabin):
330cm (130in)
Baumraum, Germany
www.baumraum.de

(above)
**Treehouse, Between
Magnolia and Pine**
Baumraum
Oak, stainless steel
H (terrace):
300cm (118in)
H (house):
400cm (157in)
W (house):
400cm (157in)
L (house):
400cm (157in)
Baumraum, Germany
www.baumraum.de

(right)
**Treehouse,
Peartreehouse**
Baumraum
Larch, plywood, steel
H: 400cm (157in)
L: 450cm (177in)
Baumraum, Germany
www.baumraum.de

(above)
**Treehouse,
World of Living**
Baumraum
Oak, larch, stainless
steel, zinc
H (terrace):
500cm (196in)
H (cabin):
650cm (256in)
W (cabin):
390cm (154in)
L (cabin):
580cm (228in)
Baumraum, Germany
www.baumraum.de

(above, above
right and right)
**Tree house,
4treehouse**
Lukasz Kos
Pine, cedar, douglas fir
H: 975cm (384in)
W: 244cm (96in)
L: 488cm (192in)
Lukasz Kos, Canada
www.studiolukaszkos.com

(right)
Outdoor room, Cube
The Garden Escape Ltd
Western red cedar
W: 400cm (157in)
L: 400cm (157in)
The Garden Escape, UK
www.thegardenescape.
co.uk

(left)
Modular home, Trio
Andy Thompson,
Sustain Design
Studio Ltd
FSC-certified
western red cedar
rainscreen cladding
W. 36.6m (120ft)
L: 103.6m (340ft)
Sustain Design Studio
Ltd, Canada
www.sustain.ca

(above)
**Portable house,
Flake House**
Olgga Architects
Wood
H: 280–320cm
(110–126in)
W: 210cm (82in)
L (small part):
275cm (108in)
L (large part):
575cm (226in)
Olgga Architects,
France
www.olgga.fr

(right)
Guest house, K4
Tom Sandonato,
Will Zemba
Extruded aluminium,
SIP (structural insulated
panels), Ipê floor and
siding, corrugated
galvalume roof and
siding, plywood interior
wall finish, cement
board interior
wall finish (bath)
W: 335cm (132in)
L: 518cm (204in)
kitHAUS, US
www.kithaus.com

(above)
**Sustainable
micro-building,
little dwelle.ing**
Richard Frankland
Timber frame
structure with various
cladding materials
W: 265cm (104in)
L: 490cm (193in)
dwelle., UK
www.dwelle.co.uk

(above)
**Outdoor space with
spa, Tea House Spa**
Paolo Bonazzi
Red cedar wood
W: 360cm (141in)
L: 420cm (165in)
Exteta srl, Italy
www.exteta.it

(left)
**Outdoor building,
Type 01**
Patrick Anderson
Insulation, pressure-
treated floor frame,
galvalume corrugated
siding, metal,
aluminium, cork
H: 315cm (124in)
W: 360cm (141in)
L: 300cm (118in)
Neoshed, US
www.neoshed.com

(above)
**Prefab building,
microSTUDIO®**
Carib Daniel Martin
Wood-framed
structure with
cement-fibre exterior
panels and recycled-
plastic trim
H: 244cm (96in)
W (main unit):
244cm (96in)
L (main unit):
266cm (104in)
MFinity, LLC, US
www.m-finity.com

(above)
**Prefab building,
kitHAUS K3**
Tom Sandonato,
Will Zemba
Aluminium, structural
insulated panels,
Ipê, corrugated
galvalume, glass
W: 396cm (156in)
L: 274cm (108in)
kitHAUS, US
www.kithaus.com

(left)
**Prefab building,
microCABANA®**
Carib Daniel Martin
Wood-framed structure
with cement-fibre
exterior panels and
recycled-plastic trim
H: 244cm (96in)
W (main unit):
244cm (96in)
L (main unit):
266cm (104in)
MFinity, LLC, US
www.m-finity.com

(above)
**Modular dwelling,
MD 42**
Edgar Blazona,
Brice Gamble
Glass, wood
W: 183cm (72in)
L: 244cm (96in)
Modular Dwellings, US
www.modulardwellings.co

(above)
**Sustainable cabin,
Williams Cabin**
Stephen Atkinson
Wood, plywood,
concrete, metal
W: 366cm (144in)
L: 366cm (144in)
Stephen Atkinson
Architecture, US
www.studioatkinson.com

(above)
**Pre-fab backyard
studio, Studio Shed**
Ryan Smith
Hardi Plank, metal roof
H: 305cm (120in)
W: 366cm (144in)
D: 305cm (120in)
Modern-Shed, US
www.modern-shed.com

(right)
**Garden building,
Verona B**
Hillhout Bergenco BV
Spruce
H: 240cm (94in)
W: 240cm (94in)
D: 240cm (94in)
Hillhout Bergenco BV,
the Netherlands
www.hillhout.com

(facing page)
**Spherical
treehouse, Eryn**
Tom Chudleigh
Fibreglass, wood
H: 320cm (126in)
Diam: 320cm (126in)
Free Spirit Spheres, Cana
www.freespiritspheres.c

(right)
**Home office/studio,
The Orb™**
David Miller, The Orb
Glass, wood, metal
W: 300cm (118in)
L: 400cm (157in)
The Orb, UK
www.theorb.biz

(above)
Outdoor room, Curve
The Garden Escape Ltd
Copper clad
W: 400cm (157in)
L: 700cm (275in)
The Garden Escape, UK
www.thegardenescape.co.uk

(right)
**Outdoor sauna,
Barrel Cedar Sauna**
Northern Lights Cedar
Tubs and Saunas
Clear western red cedar
H: 213cm (84in)
W: 213cm (84in)
L: 213 or 244cm
(84 or 96in)
Northern Lights Cedar
Tubs Inc, Canada
www.cedarbarrelsaunas.com

(right)
**Garden structure,
Outdoor Sauna**
Charlie Whinney
Steam-bent wood (oak
and ash), sheep wool,
sauna heater
H: 340cm (133in)
W: 300cm (118in)
L: 450cm (177in)
Charlie Whinney
Associates, UK
www.charliewhinney.com

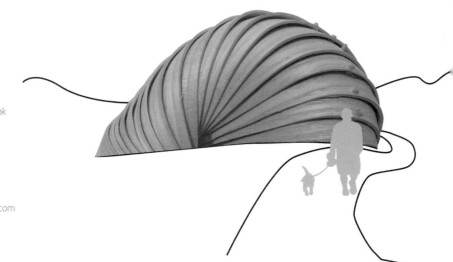

(above)
**Temporary housing
unit, Sakan Shell
Structure**
Kiwamu Yanagisawa,
Kazuya Morita, Yuki
Ozawa, Naohiko
Yamamoto
Glass fibre-reinforced
concrete
H: 300cm (118in)
W: 300cm (118in)
D: 300cm (118in)
Diam: 360cm (141in)
Sakan Shell Structure
Study Team, Japan
www.morita-arch.com

(right)
**Garden structure,
Rolling Summer House**
Charlie Whinney
Steam-bent wood
(oak and ash)
H: 300cm (118in)
Diam: 300cm (118in)
Charlie Whinney
Associates, UK
www.charliewhinney.com

(above)
Treehouse, O2
Dustin Feider
Wood, steel, plastic
H: 427–610cm
(168–240in)
O2 Treehouse, US
www.o2treehouse.com

(above and left)
**Inflatable bar
structure, Luna**
Inflate
Rip-stop nylon
H: 260cm (102in)
W: 550cm (217in)
D: 450cm (17 /in)
Inflate Products Ltd, UK
www.inflate.co.uk

(right)
**Enclosed space
for fire, storytelling
and playing,
Outdoor Fireplace**
Haugen/Zohar
Arkitekter
Wood
H: 450cm (177in)
W: 520cm (204in)
Haugen/Zohar
Arkitekter, Norway
www.hza.no

(right)
High-tech outdoor room, Bedouin Bedroom
Elena Colombo
Lightweight, durable fabric
H: 213cm (84in)
W: 183cm (72in)
L: 183cm (72in)
Colombo Construction Corp., US
www.firefeatures.com

(above)
Garden pavilion/ summer house/ children's home, Eco Capsule
Igor Zacek, Tomas Zacek
Construction timber, recycled cans
W: 560cm (220in)
Nice Architects Ltd., Slovakia
www.nicearchitects.sk

(right)
Self-sufficient living unit, Alpine Capsule
Ross Lovegrove
Clear acrylic, mirror coating
H (entrance): 100cm (39in)
Ross Lovegrove Studio, UK
www.rosslovegrove.com

(above)
**Geodesic dome,
Solardome® Retreat**
Solardome
Industries Ltd
Glass, polyester,
powder-coated,
exterior-grade
aluminium
H: 340cm (133in)
Diam: 611cm (241in)
Solardome Industries
Ltd, UK
www.solardome.co.uk

(left)
**Portable geodesic
dome, Shelter Dome**
Asha Deliverance
Steel tubing,
architectural fabric
H: 42.7 or 61m
(140 or 200ft)
Diam: 73.2 or
109.7m
(240 or 360ft)
Pacific Domes, US
www.pacificdomes.com

(above)
Living unit, LoftCube
Studio Aisslinger
Steel, glass
H: 350cm (138in)
W: 725cm (285in)
D: 725cm (285in)
LoftCube GmbH,
Germany
www.loftcube.net

(left)
**Modular office
with fitted desk
and storage (chair
optional), OfficePOD**
Tate + Hindle
Insulated fibreglass
panels, natural cork,
aluminium, LED lighting
H: 237cm (93cm)
W: 225cm (88in)
D: 225cm (88in)
OfficePOD, UK
www.officepod.co.uk

(left)
**Garden studio,
QC 2 Lo-Line
Garden Studio**
Alex Booth,
Brian Connellan
UPVC, galvanized steel
H: 250cm (98in)
W: 366cm (144in)
L: 305cm (120in)
Booths Garden
Studios, UK
www.boothsgardenstudios.co.uk

(above)
Mobile eco second home, M. E. S. H
Sanei Hopkins
Architects
Corrugated plastic,
corrugated steel, pine,
timber, tarpaulin
H: 360cm (141in)
L: 300cm (118in)
D: 110cm (43in)
Sanei Hopkins
Architects, UK
www.saneihopkins.co.uk

(above)
**Pergola, Nordfjell
Collection**
Ulf Nordfjell
Galvanized steel
H: 250 or 280cm
(98 or 110in)
W. 200 or 240cm
(78 or 94in)
Nola, Sweden
www.nola.se

(left)
**Prefabricated pod,
AirPod**
Nick Crosbie,
Roddy Mac
Plywood, aluminium,
glass, PVC
H: 280cm (110in)
W: 300cm (118in)
D: 400cm (157in)
Inflate, UK
www.inflate.co.uk
www.airclad.com

(left and above)
**Micro compact
house, Paco**
Jo Nagasaka +
Schemata
Architecture Office
Wood, FRP
H: 282cm (111in)
W: 282cm (111in)
L: 282cm (111in)
D: 282cm (111in)
Schemata Architecture
Office, Japan
www.sschemata.com

(right)
**Residential studio,
Spacebox®**
Mart de Jong
High-grade composites
H: 280cm (110in)
W: 300cm (118in)
L: 650cm (256in)
HCI, the Netherlands
www.spacebox.nl

Jun Ueno

As living space becomes more expensive, particularly in large cities, it is no surprise that we are prizing outside space more highly, or that architects are developing new types of buildings to suit our changing needs and lifestyles.

Once no more than functional eyesores, hidden from sight, traditional outdoor structures – from the ubiquitous garden sheds to *faux* Tyrolean summerhouses – have undergone a complete metamorphosis in recent years, namely Modernism. Today, instead of rustic un-chic structures, outdoor space can be constructed in myriad materials and used for countless applications, from office and exercise spaces to artists' studios and spare rooms. These new structures are sophisticated architectural features that give new focus to whatever area you call your outside space.

One such design that particularly captures the zeitgeist is the aptly named Magic Box, designed by the Japanese architect Jun Ueno, whose Magic Box company was established in Los Angeles in 2005. Ueno studied art and architecture at Nihon University, Tokyo, and these two disciplines, together with a real understanding of the dynamic relationship that can be created between architecture and landscape, define his work. Magic Box, his signature piece, is the ultimate flexible twenty-first-century shelter; as he explains, "I had been interested in temporary architecture since I was young, and I have been designing various prefabricated structures since then. I wanted to create temporary architecture that is semi-permanent, but that can be useful and beneficial to everyone. What I really wanted to do was to design a space that was so impersonal it could have multiple uses and the user could be part of the building process by deciding exactly what they wanted their space for. I only put 50 per cent of my expression into the work, and leave the other 50 per cent to the user. I had four criteria for the design: 1) that it could be located anywhere; 2) that it could be used in a wide range of applications; 3) that the interior provided a deep level of comfort; and 4) provided an environment that no one ever has experienced before."

Constructed of powder-coated stainless steel and glass and made to measure, Magic Box is a flexible concept that can range in size from a small kiosk to an entire home – its applications are limitless. It can be placed in any outside context and can also be used in the interior – with the optional installation of electricity and water lines; it can be used as a residence or a resort home.

Commercially, it can be used as a café, restaurant or office.

The design concept owes much to Ueno's heritage. "I have always been interested in the frames used in historical buildings such as Katsura-Rikyu, the Katsura Imperial Villa and Kinkaku-ji, the Temple of the Golden Pavilion, both types of traditional Japanese wooden architecture," he explains. "I think these structures are equally beautiful viewed from inside or outside and this is what I've aimed for with the design of Magic Box. Further, inspiration, implemented in the design came from origami, the traditional Japanese art of paper folding, which lends the structure its delicate, decorative design."

Magic Box also has strong sculptural qualities. Ueno worked in the studio of the Japanese impressionist sculptor, Nobuo Sekine, who produced a lot of environmental art, though, philosophically, as Ueno says, "My desire is to create a new concept, something that doesn't fit either the categories of art or architecture." His solution is a fusion of these two disciplines with the pierced glass apertures on all sides abstracting and transforming a familiar form into an extraordinary one, creating a pleasing balance of function and beauty. "I wanted the design to be 'simple,'" he explains, "and to have little uniqueness of character, a design that makes events happening inside the Box visually stand out."

Ueno agrees that design of outside space, in general, has become far more appealing in recent years. He feels that we live increasingly stressed lives and that we need, "to take in the beauty of nature in our lifestyles or in our workplace" as part of a healing, restorative process. Ueno is currently working on a landscape design, to complement the Magic Box and to enhance its therapeutic qualities.

(above)
Prefab architecture, Magic Box
Jun Ueno
Steel,
double-glazed glass
H: 300cm (118in)
W: 300cm (118in)
D: 300cm (118in)
Magic Box Inc, US
www.magicboxincusa.com

(above)
**Modular dwelling,
MD 144**
Edgar Blazona
Steel, translucent
fibreglass
W: 366cm (144in)
L: 366cm (144in)
Modular Dwellings, US
www.modulardwellings.co

(above)
**Bespoke designs,
O2 Arena**
The Garden Escape Ltd
Cedar cladding, zinc
cladding around
the roof overhang,
powder-coated
aluminium doors and
window frames
W: 6m (19⅝ft)
L: 18m (59ft)
The Garden Escape, UK
www.thegardenescape.
co.uk

(right)
**Prefab building,
microSHED®**
Carib Daniel Martin
Wood-framed
structure with
cement-fibre
exterior panels and
recycled-plastic trim
H: 244cm (96in)
W (main unit):
244cm (96in)
L (main unit):
266cm (104in)
MFinity, LLC, US
www.m-finity.com

(above and above right)
Accessory building, Mandeville Canyon Treehouse
Christopher Kempel, Rockefeller Partners Architects
Concrete, painted steel, stainless steel, wood, glass
W: 300cm (118in)
L: 550cm (217in)
Rockefeller Partners Architects, US
www.rockefeller-pa.com

(right)
House, House H
Bevk Perovic Arhitekti
Concrete
H (max): 425cm (167in)
H (min): 325cm (128in)
W (max): 609cm (240in)
L (max): 1329cm (523in)
Bevk Perovic Arhitekti, Slovenia
www.bevkperovic.com

(right)
Guest house, LVM
Rocio Romero
Copper-coloured
sheet metal, glass and
two-wall panel system
H: 343cm (135in)
W: 765cm (301in)
D: 765cm (301in)
Rocio Romero LLC, US
www.rocioromero.com

(above)
Pavilion
Richard Schultz
Stainless steel with
pleated vinyl mesh
top and side curtains
W: 305cm (120in)
L: 305cm (120in)
Richard Schultz, US
www.richardschultz.com

(right)
**Summerhouse (in the
shape of a life-sized
excavator, covered
with green climbing
plants), Green Oasis**
Studio Jo Meesters
in collaboration with
Marije van der Park
Powder-coated steel
H: 397cm (156in)
W: 249cm (98in)
L: 732cm (288in)
Studio Jo Meesters,
the Netherlands
www.jomeesters.nl

(above)
Gazebo, Pergola
Frassinago Lab
Satin stainless steel,
slats of stratified
material, technical
fabric for outdoors
H: 250cm (98in)
W: 340cm (133in)
L: 340cm (133in)
Coro, Italy
www.coroitalia.it

(above)
Daybed
José A. Gandia-Blasco
Anodized aluminium,
fabric, polyurethane
foam rubber
H: 205cm (80in)
W: 205cm (80in)
D: 205cm (80in)
Gandiablasco, Spain
www.gandiablasco.com

(right)
Pergola, Módulo
José A. Gandia-Blasco
Anodized aluminium,
canvas on plastic fabric
H: 250cm (98in)
W: 246cm (97in)
D: 246cm (97in)
Gandiablasco, Spain
www.gandiablasco.com

(right)
Retractable coverage system for the protection from sun and rain, Impact
R&D Corradi
Aluminium runners,
PVC folding canvas
Various dimensions
Corradi, Italy
www.corradi.eu

(above)
Retractable coverage system, Pergotenda® Iridium
R&D Corradi
Aluminium, PVC
folding canvas
Made to order
Corradi, Italy
www.corradi.eu

(right)
Vertical awning, VertiTex
Weinor
Translucent fabrics of the Soltis® collection
H: 240cm (94in)
W: 600cm (236in)
Weinor GmbH & Co. KG, Germany
www.weinor.de/
www.weinor.com

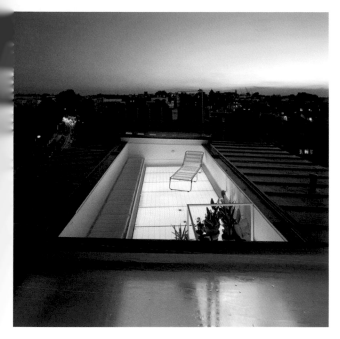

(above)
**Roof garden,
Garden Apartment**
Gianni Botsford
White powder-coated
steel grating (flooring),
white powder-coated
mild steel (staircase
and railings), white resin
(bench), retractable
glass and steel
(sliding skylight)
W: 320cm (126in)
L: 750cm (295in)
Gianni Botsford
Architects, UK
www.giannibotsford.com

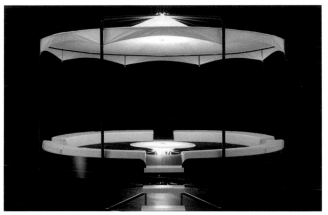

(right)
**Lounging furniture,
BeHive**
Dirk Wynants
Airtex, synthetic
leather
Light set for table
and lamp (220 V)
H: 300cm (118in)
Diam: 400cm (157in)
Extremis, Belgium
www.extremis.be

(left)
**Parasoleil panels,
Kenyan**
Uriah Bueller
90% recycled
solid copper
Custom-sized
Parasoleil, US
www.parasoleil.com

(above)
**Parasoleil panels,
Flanigan**
Uriah Bueller
90% recycled
solid copper
Custom-sized
Parasoleil, US
www.parasoleil.com

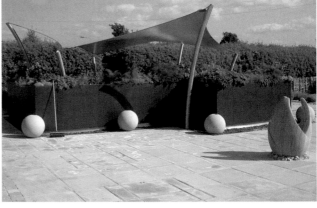

(left)
**Automatic
shading system,
SunSquare Sunsail**
Mag. Gerald Wurz
Stainless steel, canvas
with Sattler 321
Panama
H: 250–400cm
(98–157in)
W (max):
700cm (275in)
L (max):
700cm (275in)
SunSquare Kautzky
GmbH, Austria
www.sunsquare.com

(above)
**Tensile-fabric shade
structure, Chelsea**
Colin Puttick
Marine-quality
stainless steel,
lacquered PVC/PES
membrane
H: 320cm (126in)
W: 750cm (295in)
L: 750cm (295in)
Arc-Can Shade
Structures Ltd, UK
www.arccan.co.uk

(right)
Automatically shading system, SunSquare Sunsail
Mag. Gerald Wurz
Stainless steel, canvas with Sattler 321 Panama
H: 250-400cm (98-157in)
W (max): 700cm (275in)
L (max): 700cm (275in)
SunSquare Kautzky GmbH, Austria
www.sunsquare.com

(above)
Tensile-fabric shade structure, Curzon AH2400
Colin Puttick
Marine-quality stainless steel, lacquered PVC/PES membrane
H: 320cm (126in)
W: 425cm (167in)
L: 468cm (184in)
Arc-Can Shade Structures Ltd, UK
www.arccan.co.uk

(left)
Tensile fabric shade structure, Curzon AH5000
Colin Puttick
Powder-coated steel, lacquered PVC/PES membrane
H: 340cm (133in)
W: 608cm (239in)
L: 608cm (239in)
Arc-Can Shade Structures Ltd, UK
www.arccan.co.uk

(right)
Tensile-fabric shade structure, Concord CPH4000L
Colin Puttick
Marine-quality stainless steel, lacquered PVC/PES membrane
H: 320cm (126in)
W: 678cm (267in)
L: 798cm (314in)
Arc-Can Shade Structures Ltd, UK
www.arccan.co.uk

(right)
**Shade-maker,
Camerarius**
Markus Boge,
Patrick Frey
Stainless steel,
polyester fabric
H (rod): 300cm (118in)
W (one shade-sail):
90cm (35in)
L (one shade-sail):
120cm (47in)
Skia GmbH, Germany
www.skia.de

(above)
**Shade leaf,
Rimbou Venus**
Pieter Willemyns
Aluminium, stainless
steel, fabric
H: 220cm (86in)
W: 130cm (51in)
Umbrosa NV, Belgium
www.umbrosa.be

(right)
**Sun sail, Butterfly
by Sunsquare**
Gerald Wurz
Stainless steel,
sailcloth (acryl)
W: 540cm (212in)
L: 540cm (212in)
Viteo Outdoors, Austria
www.viteo.at

(left)
**Luminous parasol,
Juri G**
Studio Vertijet
Polyester,
stainless steel
LED, 220V (RGB-
changeable colour)
H: 300cm (118in)
Diam: 310cm (122in)
Skia GmbH, Germany
www.skia.de

(above)
Parasol, Tornado
Klaus Weihe
Stainless steel, PVC
H: 329 or 370cm
(130 or 146in)
W: 280 or 420cm
(110 or 165in)
Length: 280
or 420cm
(110 or 165in)
Tradewinds Parasol,
South Africa
www.tradewinds.co.za

(left)
Pulpit, Oris
Dirk Wynants
Aluminium
H: 260cm (102in)
Diam: 260cm (102in)
Extremis, Belgium
www.extremis.be

(right)
**Wall-mounted
parasol, Paraflex**
Peter Leleu
Aluminium, stainless
steel, Olefine
Diam: 270cm (106in)
Umbrosa, Belgium
www.umbrosa.be
www.globalparasols.com

(facing page)
**Folding parasol,
Ensombra Parasol**
Odosdesign
Galvanized
thermo-lacquered
iron, thermo-lacqured
stainless steel,
phenolic plate
H: 212cm (83in)
Diam: 180 or
210cm (70 or 82in)
Gandiablasco, Spain
www.gandiablasco.com

(above)
**Cantilever parasol,
Ocean Master MAX
Cantilever Classic**
Dougan Clarke
Marine-grade
aluminium,
stainless steel
H (when open):
259cm (102in)
Diam: 396cm (156in)
Tuuci, US
www.tuuci.com

(right)
**Shade maker,
Silhouette**
Woodline
Aluminium, stainless
steel, sunbrella canopy
H: 245cm (96in)
W: 300cm (118in)
L: 500cm (196in)
Woodline, South Africa
www.woodline.co.za

(left)
Parasol, Nenufar
Yonoh
Laquered aluminium
(Fabric: Batyline
Ferrari Group)
H: 220cm (86in)
W (base): 48cm
(18⅞in)
Samoa, Spain
www.samoadesign.com

(below)
**Parasol, Ocean
Master Classic
Autoscope**
Dougan Clarke
Marine-grade
aluminium with
patented modular
operating system
H (when open):
259cm (102in)
Diam: 396cm (156in)
Tuuci, US
www.tuuci.com

(above)
Parasol, Breezer
Davy Grosemans
Polyester, pvc-coated
acrylic fabric, stainless
steel, anodized and
powder-coated
aluminium
H: 245cm (96in)
W: 250cm (98in)
L: 350cm (138in)
Symo NV, Belgium
www.symo.be

(right)
Parasol,
Shadylace parasol
Chris Kabel
Polyester, wood
H: 235cm (92in)
Diam: 210cm (82in)
Droog BV, the
Netherlands
www.droog.com

(above)
Sunshade, Branch
Ilaria Marelli
Varnished metal
H: 250cm (98in)
W: 225cm (88in)
D: 145cm (57in)
Coro Italia, Italy
www.coroitalia.it

(left)
Umbrella, Multivola
Self-opening
Windproof Umbrella
Surinder Jindal
Stainless steel,
aluminium,
water-repellent
polyester fabric
Diam: 240cm (94in)
Loom Crafts Furniture
Pvt Ltd, India
www.loomcrafts.com

Art for gardens

(above)
**Pavilion, Golden
Jewel Box**
Angela Fritsch
Architekten
Lasered aluminium
sheet
H: 300cm (118in)
W: 644cm (254in)
L: 937cm (369in)
Angela Fritsch
Architekten, Germany
www.af-architekten.de

(above)
Wall piece, Untitled
Alexander Beleschenko
Toughened laminate
glass with
painted enamels
H: 297cm (117in)
W: 300cm (118in)
D: 1.5cm (⅝in)
Alexander
Beleschenko, UK
www.beleschenko.com

(right)
Screen, Palm
Natasha Webb
Brushed stainless steel
H: 140cm (55in)
W: 120cm (47in)
D: 3mm (⅛in)
Design to Grace, UK
www.designtograce.co.uk

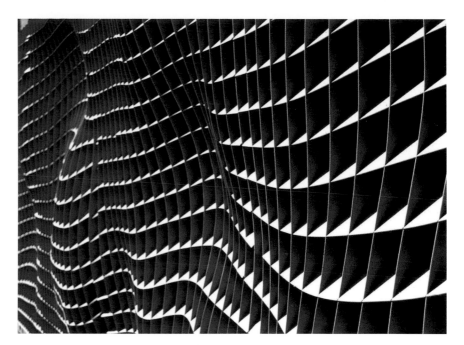

(above)
**Screen, Serpent
and Sun 1**
Wally Gilbert
Ductile cast iron
H (each individual
panel): 122cm (48in)
W (each individual
panel): 86cm (34in)
D: 2.5cm (1in)
Wally Gilbert, UK
www.wallygilbert.co.uk

(right)
**Balcony Panel,
Veil of Summer**
Natasha Webb
Brushed stainless steel
H: 150cm (59in)
W: 120cm (49in)
D: 4mm (⅛in)
To Grace, UK
www.designtograce.co.uk

(left)
**Metal wall art,
Make a Wish**
Garth Williams
Stainless steel, wax
H: 60cm (23in)
W: 60cm (23in)
Edge Company, UK
www.edgecompany.
co.uk
www.gardenbeet.com

(above)
**Railings, Hand-forged
Contemporary Railings**
Bushy Park Ironworks
Zinc finish
H (railings):
100cm (39in)
II (newel posts):
140–170cm
(55–66in)
Bushy Park
Ironworks, Ireland
www.bushyparkironworks.com

(right)
Fence/panel, Rusted Flower Fencing
Secret Gardens Furniture
Hand-forged rusted metal
H: 120cm (47in)
W: 100cm (39in)
Secret Gardens Furniture, UK
www.secretgardens furniture.com

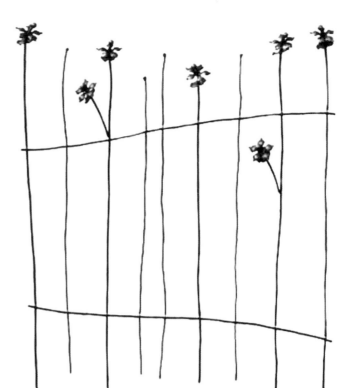

(below)
Gate, Dried Earth and Heat Haze
Tim Fortune
Mild steel
H: 180cm (70in)
W: 80cm (31in)
Tim Fortune, UK
www.timfortune.com

(right)
Gate, Mowbray Park Gate
Wendy Ramshaw
Mild steel, glass, industrial paint
H: 300cm (118in)
W: 500cm (196in)
D: 12cm (4¾in)
Wendy Ramshaw, UK
www.ramshaw-watkins.com

(right)
Pierced window panels, Batley Wall
Alyosha Moeran, Amy Douglas, Guy Stevens
Ancaster blue beige limestone
H: 90cm (35in)
W: 200cm (78in)
Alyosha Moeran, UK
www.alyoshamoeran.co.uk

(left)
Relief carving, Batley Wall
Alyosha Moeran, Amy Douglas, Guy Stevens
Sandstone (Yorkstone)
H: 5m (16½ft)
W: 10m (33ft)
Alyosha Moeran, UK
www.alyoshamoeran.co.uk

(left)
Garden Mosaic, Pebble Mosaic
Maggy Howarth
Green slate strips, mixed Scottish granite pebbles, bright yellow, white quartz pebbles
Diam: 250cm (98in)
D: 7.5cm (3in)
Maggy Howarth, UK
www.maggyhowarth.co.uk

(above)
Drystone wall sculpture, Giant's Seat
Donald Gunn
Reclaimed stone
H: 130cm (51in)
H (seat base): 70cm (27in)
L: 900cm (354in)
Donald Gunn, UK
www.drystone-walls.com

(above)
**Inscription,
Archimedes' Blues II**
Gary Breeze
Welsh slate
H: 22cm (8⅝in)
L: 98cm (38in)
D: 2cm (¾in)
Gary Breeze, UK
www.garybreeze.co.uk

(right)
**Pond cover,
Decorative Pond
Cover, Prior's
Court School**
Wendy Ramshaw
Anodized aluminium
W: 180cm (70in)
L: 360m (141in)
D: 2cm (¾in)
Wendy Ramshaw, UK
www.ramshaw-
watkins.com

(above)
**Gate, Pilsdon Pen
Gate and Stile**
Karen Hansen
English oak
H: 110cm (43in)
W: 330cm (130in)
Karen Hansen, UK
www.karenhansen.co.uk

(left)
**Garden Mosaic,
Life Mosaic**
Maggy Howarth
Pebbles
Area: 28m² (301ft²)
Maggy Howarth, UK
www.maggyhowarth.co.uk

(right)
**Glass sculptures,
Temperate House
Persian Pond,
Royal Botanic
Gardens, Kew**
Dale Chihuly
Handblown glass
Chihuly Studio, US
www.chihuly.com

(above)
**Garden décor,
Bird-shaped Fence
Post Protector**
Powder-coated metal
Wren/Robin: 6 x 6cm
(2⅜ x 2⅜in)
Thrush/Blackbird:
7 x 7cm (2¾ x 2¾in)
The Worm
That Turned, UK
www.worm.co.uk

(right)
**Decorative
metalwork, Fish**
Mike Savage
Copper and aluminium
H: 100cm (39in)
L: 30cm (11¾in)
Mike Savage, UK
www.
mikesavagesculptor.
blogspot.com

(left)
Garden sculpture,
Butterfly Screen
Yasemen Hussein
Glass, Perspex,
lead, steel
H: 183cm (72in)
W: 183cm (72in)
Yasemen Hussein, UK
www.yasemenhussein.com

(above)
Installation,
Field of Infinity
Inge Panneels
Cast glass, steel
H: 120cm (47in)
Diam: 10cm (3⅞in)
Inge Panneels, UK
www.idagos.co.uk

(left)
Garden sculpture, Vigil
Jonathan Garratt
Wood-fired ceramic,
stainless steel
W (individual):
6cm (2⅜in)
L (individual):
6cm (2⅜in)
Jonathan Garratt, UK
www.jonathangarratt.com

(right)
**Glass sculpture,
Olympia Tree**
Neil Wilkin
Forged and textured,
marine-grade stainless
steel, solid glass
tri-drops
H: 350cm (138in)
W: 300cm (118in)
Diam: 300cm (118in)
Neil Wilkin, UK
www.neilwilkin.com

(above)
**Garden sculpture,
Cirrus**
John Creed
Stainless steel
H: 200cm (78in)
John Creed, UK
www.creedmetalwork.com

(right)
**Garden sculpture,
Cumulus**
John Creed
Stainless steel
H: 200cm (78in)
John Creed, UK
www.creedmetalwork.com

(left)
**Glass sculpture,
Dew Drops**
Neil Wilkin
Solid glass drops on
316 marine-grade
stainless steel
H (stems): up to
200cm (78in)
Diam: 7, 9 or 10.5cm
(2¾, 3½ or 4⅛in)
Neil Wilkin, UK
www.neilwilkin.com

(above)
**Glass sculpture,
Gold Seed Head**
Neil Wilkin
Solid glass 'petals'
with 24ct gold,
316 marine-grade
stainless steel
H: 150–220cm
(59–86in)
Diam: 60cm (23in)
Neil Wilkin, UK
www.neilwilkin.com

(right)
**Glass sculpture,
Tear Drops**
Neil Wilkin
Solid glass drops
with blown 'tear'
316 marine-grade
stainless steel
H (stems): up to
200cm (78in)
Diam: 7, 9 or 10.5cm
(2¾, 3½ or 4⅛in)
Neil Wilkin, UK
www.neilwilkin.com

(above)
**Biometric sculptures,
Island Growth**
Eberhard Bosslet
Polyurethane, fibreglass
H: 45–90cm
(17¾–35in)
Eberhard Bosslet
at VG-Bild/Kunst
and Whiteconcepts,
Germany
www.whiteconcepts.de
www.bosslet.com

(above)
Screen
Viki Govan,
Richard Warner
Galvanized mild steel
I l: 116cm (46in)
W: 33cm (13in)
D: 6mm (¼in)
Iron Vein, UK
www.ironvein.co.uk

(right)
**Rain collectors,
Releaf**
Fulguro
Lacquered aluminium
H: 63cm (24in)
Diam: 38cm (15in)
Teracrea, Italy
www.teracrea.com

(left)
Faux tree (can be used as trellis), Nest Tree
Jirachai Tangkijngamwong
Teakwood
H: 250 or 270cm (98 or 106in)
Diam: 250 or 200cm (98 or 78in)
Deesawat Industries Co., Ltd, Thailand
www.deesawat.com

(above)
Garden stakes, Fallin'
notNeutral design team
Powder-coated steel
H 38–86cm (15–34in)
notNeutral, US
www.notneutral.com

(below)
Garden stakes, Bloomin'
notNeutral design team
Powder-coated steel
H 38–86cm (15–34in)
notNeutral, US
www.notneutral.com

(above)
**Wire sculpture,
Cotswold Sheep
with Lamb**
Rupert Till
Wire netting
H: 80cm
W: 50cm
L: 120cm (47in)
Rupert Till, UK
www.ruperttill.com

(above)
Wire sculpture, Horse
Rupert Till
Steel wire
H: 210cm (82in)
W: 60cm (23in)
L: 180cm (70in)
Rupert Till, UK
www.ruperttill.com

(right)
**Wire sculpture,
Black Hens**
Celia Smith
Steel and copper wire
H: 42cm (16½in)
W: 30cm (11¾in)
Celia Smith, UK
www.celia-smith.co.uk

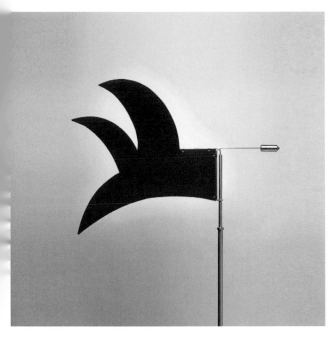

(above)
Wind vane, Red Cock
Afra and Tobia Scarpa
Aluminium,
stainless steel
H (max): 260cm
(102in)
Dimensione
Disegno srl, Italy
www.dimensione
disegno.it

(top right)
Wind vane, Blue Birds
Afra and Tobia Scarpa
Aluminium,
stainless steel
H (max):
260cm (102in)
Dimensione
Disegno srl, Italy
www.dimensione
disegno.it

(above and right)
**Laundry line,
Early Bird**
Fabian von Spreckelsen
Powder-coated steel,
galvanized and coated
steel cable, PS
H: 200cm (78in)
W: 95cm (37in)
First Aid Design,
the Netherlands
www.first-aid-design.
com

(below)
**Candle Holder,
Water Lilly (Garden
Flower Series)**
Junko Mori
Powder-coated,
forged mild steel
H: 15cm (5⅞in)
W: 29cm (11⅜in)
L: 29cm (11⅜in)
Junko Mori, UK
www.junkomori.com

(above)
Sundial, Solea
Ralph Kondermann
Stainless steel,
powder-coated steel
H: 65cm (25½in)
Diam: 37cm (14½in)
Blomus GmbH,
Germany
www.blomus.com

(right)
**Sculpture,
Her Ascension**
Ferry Staverman
Iron, thread, glue,
PVC, MDF
H: 103cm (41cm)
H (from floor):
170cm (66in)
Diam: 16cm (6¼in)
Ferry Staverman,
the Netherlands
www.ferrystaverman.nl

(above)
Sculpture, Wave
Malcolm Martin,
Gaynor Dowling
Cedar
H: 240cm (94in)
W: 30cm (11¾in)
Martin and Dowling, UK
www.martinanddowling.
co.uk

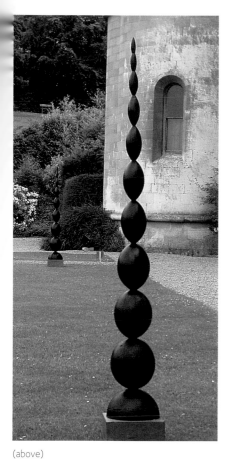

(above)
**Sculpture,
Oak Eclipse**
Barry Mason
Green oak, stainless
steel, stone
H: 220 or 260cm
(86 or 102in)
Barry Mason, UK
www.barry-mason.co.uk

(above)
**Kinetic sculpture,
Red Spiral**
Ivan Black
Stainless steel, acrylic
H: 210cm (82in)
Diam: 60cm (23in)
Ivan Black, UK
www.ivanblack.co.uk

(left)
Sculpture, Thales
Barry Mason
Mirror-polished
stainless steel
H: 280cm (110in)
Barry Mason, UK
www.harry-mason.co.uk

(above)
Sculpture, Sail
Matt Stein
Mirrored, 316
stainless steel
H: 200cm (78in)
W: 100cm (39in)
D: 50cm (19in)
Steinworks
Sculpture, UK
www.steinworks.co.uk

(above)
Sculpture, Resonance
Matt Stein
Brushed, 316
stainless steel
H: 200cm (78in)
W: 100cm (39in)
D: 50cm (19in)
Steinworks
Sculpture, UK
www.steinworks.co.uk

(right)
Sculpture, Drop Urn
Kathy Dalwood
Concrete
H: 30cm (11¾in)
Kathy Dalwood, UK
www.kathydalwood.com

(above)
**Sculpture, Nine
Satellites**
Gary Breeze
Purbeck limestone,
Welsh slate
H: 110cm (43in)
W: 45cm (17¾in)
D: 45cm (17¾in)
Diam (sphere):
30cm (11¾in)
Gary Breeze, UK
www.garybreeze.co.uk

(above)
Sculpture, Parasol
Bruce Williams
Painted steel
H: 150cm (59in)
W: 150cm (59in)
L: 150cm (59in)
Bruce Williams, UK
www.brucewilliams.net

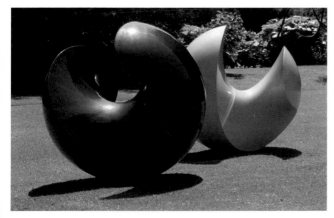

(left)
**Sculpture,
Half Sphelix**
Johnny Hawkes
Fibreglass
Diam: 92cm (36in)
PW Ltd, UK
www.sphelix.com

(above)
Seat, Corallo
Fernando and
Humberto Campana
Hand-bent steel wire
with epoxy paint
H: 90cm (35in)
H (seat): 45cm
(17¾in)
W: 100cm (39in)
L: 145cm (57in)
Edra, Italy
www.edra.com

(above)
**Sculpture/seat,
Terrazzo Seat**
Thomas Heatherwick
Polished concrete
H: 83cm (32in)
W: 75cm (29in)
L: 275cm (108in)
Heatherwick Studio, UK
www.heatherwick.com

(right)
Sculpture, Eryngium
Ruth Moilliet
Stainless steel
Diam: 150cm (59in)
Ruth Moilliet, UK
www.ruthmoilliet.com

(above)
**Art installation,
Field of Light**
Bruce Munro
Acrylic stems, glass
spheres, optic fibres,
colour-changing
projectors
Bruce Munro Ltd, UK
www.brucemunro.co.uk

(above)
Sculpture, Berry
Rebecca Newnham
Mirror, fibreglass
H: 100cm (39in)
W: 100cm (39in)
D: 100cm (39in)
Rebecca Newnham, UK
www.
rebeccanewnham.co.uk

(left)
**Bench, Winding
Bench (With
Boulders)**
Alison Crowther
Unseasoned
English oak
H: 50cm (19in)
L: 15m (49ft)
Alison Crowther, UK
www.alisoncrowther.com

(left)
Sculpture, Seedhead
Ruth Moilliet
Steel
Diam: 65–125cm
(25–49in)
Ruth Moilliet, UK
www.ruthmoilliet.com

(above)
Sculpture, Allium
Ruth Moilliet
Stainless steel
Diam: 55–200cm
(21–78¾in)
Ruth Moilliet, UK
www.ruthmoilliet.com

(facing page)
Sculpture, Syntax
Steve Tobin
Bronze
Diam: 183cm (72in)
Steve Tobin, US
www.stevetobin.com

(above)
**Light sculpture,
Glamrocks**
Peter Freeman
Sprayed concrete,
stainless steel,
colour-changing
fibreoptics
Various dimensions
Peter Freeman, UK
www.peterfreeman.co.uk

(above)
**Sculpture,
Highland Ball**
Joe Smith
Caithness slate
Diam: 180cm (70in)
Joe Smith, UK
www.joe-smith.co.uk

Andy Sturgeon

For garden designer Andy Sturgeon, art and design are essential components of his work. As he says, "If you're influenced just by gardens, you're going to be going round and round in circles. I find art and design a very useful source of inspiration, so, for example, we put a lot of architectural ideas into our gardens." In terms of inspiration, Sturgeon describes himself as "an observer". He explains: "I might see a building façade and think 'that might work in a garden context', or I might take the mood and atmosphere of a Rothko painting, or the interior of a bar or a hotel I've visited, but by putting these elements into an entirely different context you can reinvent them. It might be something about proportion you take, or about curves, or about colour; it can be very subtle."

One of Britain's best-known contemporary landscape architects and designers, Sturgeon has helped reinvigorate gardening through his imaginative designs, books, newspaper articles and lectures. He has an international clientele and, since 2004, his practice has been designing gardens for Huf Haus. Sturgeon's highly contemporary designs for urban and rural spaces use natural materials to articulate fresh new landscapes. His practice has won prestigious RHS medals at the Chelsea and Hampton Court Flower Shows, and he has been influential in encouraging new young gardeners to pick up their hoes, though he would be the first

to admit that we are tempted into our gardens by more than simply planting. "I suppose," says Sturgeon, "our gardens have become more about lifestyle and less about gardening, (that's not true of everyone, of course). To some extent, the biggest single change has been people's general awareness of design in a way that didn't exist before. If you think about TV programmes on architecture, they have really captured the public's imagination and people interested in gardens have also been drawn by that."

Thought Wall, used in Sturgeon's award-winning Cancer Research UK Garden of 2008 is a good example of the way Sturgeon uses art in a garden context. It features a decorative fence/divider composed of cut-steel pipes that form a delicate, almost filigree-like divider that casts bubble-shaped shadows across a nearby wall, complementing the delicate ferns that surround it. "In my mind," says Sturgeon of the project, "there's a '60s dress made out of odd rings, something that I'd seen and it lodged in my mind, and that was the essence of Thought Wall."

Does Sturgeon think art is ideally expressed in terms of planting and materials in the garden or does he think fine art itself has a place in the garden landscape? "It can be done," he replies, "and gardens do, on the whole, make quite good settings for sculpture, but it's an entirely different thing to integrate sculpture into a landscape. I think that planting and hard landscaping with artistry

is a better end result than just sticking any old bit of sculpture in a garden and saying 'there you go'. If you put a Henry Moore into a landscape, that Henry Moore will dominate that landscape."

"With any garden," continues Sturgeon, "it is not any one thing in isolation, but the various components and the way they work together that makes the garden successful. The availability of plants has changed tremendously in recent years – it has changed the look of our gardens. When I started doing this kind of work in the '80s, it was all shrubs, spirea and boring stuff. Now the choice of plants is colossal. Climate change has also played a part in our choices too. You could do a tropical garden now (in some parts of the UK) if you wanted to – you just wouldn't have been able to do that 20 years ago."

I ask Sturgeon whose work he admires. He answers without hesitation, "Thomas Heatherwick". Heatherwick is the young British designer whose architectural interventions in the landscape feature innovative engineering and materials. "One of the things I admire about him," says Sturgeon, "is his versatility, he can turn his hand to many things."

When I ask Sturgeon about future trends for gardens he is less enthusiastic. "The idea of innovation in gardening never sits very comfortably with me," he says. "We tend to use a lot of natural stone and timber – they're not innovative in themselves, it's the way we use them that is."

(left)
**Sculptural bench,
Fountain Bench**
Charlie Whinney
Oak
H: 290cm (114in)
W. 340cm (133in)
L: 300cm (118in)
Charlie Whinney
Associates, UK
www.charliewhinney.com

(above)
Sculpture, Roots
Steve Tobin
Bronze
H: 366cm (144in)
W: 488cm (192in)
D: 427cm (168in)
Steve Tobin, US
www.stevetobin.com

(above)
Sculpture, Alliums
Joe Smith
Welsh slate,
stainless steel
Diam: 27.5cm (11in)
Joe Smith, UK
www.joe-smith.co.uk

(right)
**Vase,
Herringbone Vase**
Joe Smith
Westmoreland slate
H: 60cm (23in)
Joe Smith, UK
www.joe-smith.co.uk

(above)
**Sculpture, Living
Willow Ball**
Lizzie Farey
Willow
Diam: 250cm (98in)
Lizzie Farey, UK
www.lizziefarey.co.uk

(above)
**Sculptures,
Yew Forms**
Laura Ellen Bacon
Willow (black maul)
H: 180cm (70in)
W: 100 and 120cm
(39 and 47in)
D: 100cm (39in)
Laura Ellen Bacon, UK
www.lauraellenbacon.com

(left)
Sculpture, Hazel Oval
Lizzie Farey
Hazel
H: 40cm (15¾in)
W: 45cm (17¾in)
L: 60cm (23in)
Lizzie Farey, UK
www.lizziefarey.co.uk

(left)
**Garden seat,
Spiral Bench**
Alison Crowther
Unseasoned
English oak
H: 30-60cm
(11¾-23in)
W (seat): 40cm
(15¾in)
Diam: 300cm (118in)
Alison Crowther, UK
www.alisoncrowther.com

(right)
**Bench, Stratiform
Bench (4-Part)**
Alison Crowther
Unseasoned English oak
H: 40cm (15¾in)
W: 50cm (19in)
L: 375cm (148in)
Alison Crowther, UK
www.alisoncrowther.com

(right)
Bench, Loveseat
Jake Phipps
Oak or cedar
H: 50cm (19in)
L: 125cm (49in)
D: 50cm (19in)
Jake Phipps, UK
www.jakephipps.com

(above)
**Double seat,
Loveseat**
Karen Hansen
English oak,
sweet chestnut
H: 140cm (55in)
W: 120cm (47in)
D: 60cm (23in)
Karen Hansen, UK
www.karenhansen.co.uk

(right)
**Seat, Broadwalk
Tree Seat**
Tim Royall
Oak
H: 90cm (35in)
Diam (outer): 200cm
(78in)
Gaze Burvill Ltd, UK
www.gazeburvill.com

Play

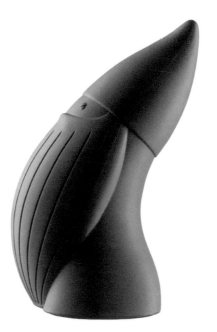
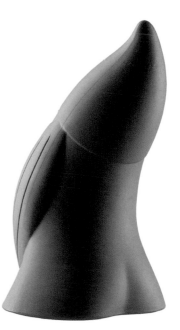

(above)
**Garden swing,
Recycled Tyre
Horse Swing**
Patrick Palumbo
Rubber tyre
H: 60cm (23in)
W: 50cm (19in)
Hen and Hammock, UK
www.henandhammock.co.uk

(above)
Swing, Keinu
Mikko Kärkkäinen
Birch wood
W: 19.5cm (7⅝in)
L: 75.5cm (29in)
D: 1cm (⅜in)
Tunto Design, Finland
www.tunto.com

(right)
**Swing, Swing
with the Plants**
Marcel Wanders
Polyethylene, rope
(the seat of the
swing can be filled
with soil and seeds
planted inside)
H: 10cm (3⅞in)
W: 75cm (29in)
D: 23cm (9in)
Droog BV, the
Netherlands
www.droog.com

(left)
Swing, Leaf Swing
Alberto Sánchez
Formica, nylon rope
H: 30cm (11¾in)
L: 70cm (27in)
D: 35cm (13¾in)
Eneastudio, Spain
www.eneastudio.com

(above)
**Lamp/swing,
Swing Lamp**
BCXSY
Polyurethane,
synthetic rope
LED light element
(runs on
rechargeable battery)
H: 6cm (2⅜in)
W: 60cm (23in)
D: 35cm (13¾in)
Slide srl, Italy
www.slidedesign.it

(left)
Swing, Light Swing
Alexander Lervik
Acrylic, stainless
steel, rope
LED lamps
H: 240cm (94in)
W: 55cm (21in)
D: 20cm (7⅞in)
SAAS instruments,
Finland
www.saas.fi

(left)
Outdoor musical instruments, Eye Chimes
Richard Cooke
Aluminium
Diam: 10cm (4in)
H; 140–270cm (55–106in)
Freenotes Ltd, UK
www.freenotes.eu

(above)
Outdoor musical instruments, The Swirl
Richard Cooke
Aluminium
W: 142cm (56in)
Freenotes Ltd, UK
www.freenotes.eu

(facing page)
Garden design, the Marshalls Garden That Kids Really Want (Chelsea Flower Show)
Ian Dexter of Lime Orchard
Lime Orchard, UK
Marshalls PLC, UK
www.limeorchard.co.uk
www.marshalls.co.uk

(left)
**Portable geodesic
dome, Playground
Dome**
Asha Deliverance
Powder-coloured
steel tubing
H: 244cm (96in)
Diam: 457cm (180in)
Pacific Domes, US
www.pacificdomes.com

(above)
**Playground,
Jungle Gym**
Sehwan Oh,
Soo Yun Ahn
Stainless steel,
polycarbonate
H: 250cm (98in)
W: 800cm (315in)
D: 400cm (157in)
OC Design studio,
Republic of Korea
www.sehwanoh.com

(right)
**Children's Seating,
Amazing Seating**
Hand Made Places
Scots pine
H: 30cm (11¾in)
W: 440cm (173in)
D: 420cm (165⅜in)
Hand Made Places
at Broxap, UK
www.handmadeplaces.co.uk

(left)
Slide, Crumpledslide
Walter Jack Studio
GRP
H: 200cm (78in)
W: 500cm (196in)
L: 500cm (196in)
D: 15cm (5⅞in)
Walter Jack Studio, UK
www.walterjack.co.uk

(above)
Climbing boulder, Castle Boulder
Playworld Systems
Pre-cast polyfibrecrete
H: 264cm (104in)
W: 142cm (56in)
L: 236cm (93in)
Playworld Systems, US
www.
playworldsystems.com

(right)
Slide, Caracool
Joel Escalona
Fibreglass, wood
H: 90cm (35in)
W: 90cm (35in)
L: 200cm (78in)
Joel Escalona, Mexico
www.joelescalona.com

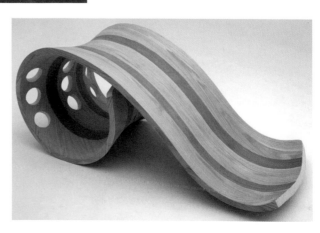

(above)
**Play sculpture,
Pig on Gate**
Hand Made Places
Scots Pine
H: 110cm (43in)
W: 150cm (59in)
D: 20cm (7⅞in)
Hand Made Places
at Broxap, UK
www.handmadeplaces.co

(above)
**Play sculpture,
Raging Bull**
Hand Made Places
Scots pine
H: 90cm (35in)
W: 170cm (66in)
D: 40cm (15¾in)
Hand Made Places
at Broxap, UK
www.handmadeplaces.co.uk

(left)
**Play sculpture/seating,
Swan Seat**
Hand Made Places
Scots pine
H: 100cm (39in)
L: 120cm (47in)
W: 110cm (43in)
Hand Made Places
at Broxap, UK
www.handmadeplaces.co.u

(above)
Seating, Atlas
Giorgio Biscaro
Polyethylene
H: 40cm (15¾in)
W: 115cm (45in)
D. 46cm (18⅛in)
Slide srl, Italy
www.slidedesign.it

(above)
Garden bench, Croco
De Overkant, Dussen
Pine
H: 60cm (23in)
W: 30cm (11¾in)
L: 160cm (63in)
Freeline International
BV, the Netherlands
www.enjoyfreeline.com

(right)
**Garden bench,
Bambisitter**
De Overkant,
Dussen
Pine
H: 35 or 75cm
(13¾ or 29in)
L: 100 or 140cm
(39 or 55in)
Freeline International
BV, the Netherlands
www.enjoyfreeline.com

(right)
**Children's outdoor
table and chair, BBO2
Table & Chairs**
Loll Designs and
notNeutral
100% post-consumer
recycled plastic
H (table): 46cm (18in)
H (chair): 58cm (23in)
W (table): 81cm (32in)
W (chair): 34cm
(13¼in)
D (table): 81cm (32in)
D (chair): 47cm
(18½in)
Loll Designs, US
www.lolldesigns.com

(above)
Children's chairs, Cub
Daniel Michalik
100%
recycled cork
H: 46cm (18in)
W: 33cm (13in)
D: 33cm (13in)
DMFD Studio, US
www.danielmichalik.com

(above)
**Children's
chaise longue,
Polyester Shell**
Erik Vandewalle
Polyester
W: 77cm (30in)
L: 170cm (66in)
Domani, Belgium
www.domani.be

(left)
**Children's rocking
chair, Italic Kid Chair**
Aluminium,
Polyethylene fibre, teak
wooden beams
Robin Delaere
H: 53cm (20in)
W: 36cm (14⅛in)
L: 56cm (22in)
Some, Belgium
www.some.be

(left and right)
**Children's armchair,
My First Translation**
Alain Gilles
Rotation-moulded,
low-density
polyethylene
H: 49.1cm (19¼in)
W: 51.6cm (20in)
D: 48cm (18⅞in)
Qui est Paul?, France
www.qui-est-paul.com

(above)
**Children's chair,
Kapsule Chair**
Karim Rashid
Injection-moulded
polypropylene
H: 46cm (18in)
W: 48cm (19in)
D: 53cm (21in)
Offi, US
www.offi.com

(above)
**Children's outdoor
chair, Kid's
Adirondack**
Loll Designs
100% post-consumer
recycled plastic
H: 58cm (22¾in)
W: 48cm (18¾in)
D: 65cm (25¾in)
Loll Designs, US
www.lolldesigns.com

(left)
**Stacking children's
chair, Alma**
Javier Mariscal
Polypropylene,
glass fibre
H: 58cm (22in)
H (seat): 32cm
(12⅝in)
W: 39cm (15⅜in)
D: 40cm (15¾in)
Magis SpA, Italy
www.magisdesign.com

(above)
Children's chair, Julian
Javier Mariscal
Rotation-moulded polyethylene
H: 55cm (21in)
H (seat): 30cm (11¾in)
W: 36cm (14⅛in)
L: 49cm (19¼in)
Magis SpA, Italy
www.magismetoo.com

(above)
Multi-purpose object, Mico
El Ultimo Grito
Rotation-moulded polyethylene
H: 40cm (15¾in)
W: 67cm (26in)
L: 67cm (26in)
Magis SpA, Italy
www.magismetoo.com

(left and above)
Children's chair/ rocker, Trioli
Eero Aarnio
Rotation-moulded polyethylene
H: 58cm (22in)
H (rocker): 45cm (17¾in)
Magis SpA, Italy
www.magismetoo.com

(left)
Abstract plastic dog, Puppy
Eero Aarnio
Rotation-moulded
polyethylene
H: 34.5, 45, 55.5
or 80.5cm (13¾,
17¾, 22 or 31in)
L: 42.5, 56.5, 69.5
or 102.5cm (16⅞, 22,
27 or 40in)
Magis SA, Italy
www.magismetoo.com

Alberto Perazza

Traditionally, children's products have tended to be scaled-down versions of designs for adults – think moulded plastic, mini versions of adult garden furniture. But this situation has changed dramatically in the last decade or so and one company, Magis, has played a major part in not only stimulating, but also transforming this market.

Very much a family business, the north Italian company Magis was founded in 1976 by Eugenio Perazza, now president. His son Alberto now heads this innovative, multi-award-winning design and manufacturing business. Magis has built a reputation for translating cutting-edge technology into mass production. It was one of the first companies to use plastic and advanced moulding technologies and technique for its products. The company has always harnessed the talents of original international designers and seems to have an intuitive talent for matching the right designer to the right project. Konstantin Grcic, Richard Sapper, Jasper Morrison, Stefano Giovannoni, Marc Newson and Ron Arad are but a few of its current stable to produce innovative design across a wide range of products, both interior and exterior. Increasingly, though, these boundaries are blurred, as Alberto Perazza explains, "At Magis it's not always easy to find a distinction between what is indoor and what is outdoor – we design flexible furniture. Products designed for indoors can be used outdoors and vice versa." A similar situation exists between the company's contract and domestic ranges.

In 2004, recognizing a gap in the market, Perazza launched the Me Too Collection, a range of furniture and toys (the Magis Puppy designed by Eero Aarnio, probably being the most instantly recognizable product in the range) specifically designed for children between the ages of two and six years. Perazza, the intellect behind the collection, did not want mini versions of adult designs, but designs especially for children. The company set out to redefine the concept of children's products and employed child specialists, such as Edward Melhuish, Professor of Child Development at the University of London, to ensure designs had an educational value – and encouraged play and development. Why this sudden interest in children's products? "Parents," Perazza replies, "are prepared to spend more on children's items. I think the market is expanding year by year because I think there is more attention paid to the child's environment, to their linguistic, social, emotional and intellectual development than before."

Designers for Me Too were cherry-picked for their talent for such design. "Javier Mariscal," says Perazza, offering an example, "is more like a graphic designer, a cartoonist rather than an industrial designer and his background helped us develop the right products for the children. Also Eero Aarnio has been involved since day one of Me Too. We approached these two designers first by looking at their existing designs and we thought their design language appropriate for designing for children."

Perazza continues: "With Me Too we wanted to do things in the way children themselves might design their own toys and furniture – this is reflected in the name of the collection, which is the voice of the child demanding to have their own objects, their own work which is different to the adult's world. Because," he says, "children use furniture differently to adults. Take a chair and reduce it in scale and it's asking the child to be too like Mama and Papa – it's like dressing your kids as a mini version of yourself. It's wrong." He cites the Trioli chair designed by the Finnish designer Eero Aarnio, (winner of the Compasso D'Oro prize) as an example of the Me Too range. This is an upside-down chair that allows three different seating positions, and, if you turn it upside down instantly it becomes a rocker. "We have to bear in mind," says Perazza, "children grow very quickly from two to six, and you need to find ways to make things adaptable – to grow with the child and find ways of engaging children."

Magis also design a range of other products for outdoors including bird houses, dog houses and, of course, furniture. Perazza explains, "We now do a lot of products that are suitable for outdoor use. We believe this is a market that is expanding rapidly – people tend to spend more time outdoors these days and probably will in the future. This is a market we're continuing to research and develop."

(above)
**Modular play
furniture, K-block**
El Ultimo Grito
Polyethylene
H: 77.5cm (30in)
H (seat): 41cm
(16⅛in)
W: 47cm (18½in)
Nola, Sweden
www.nola.se

(above)
Stool, MOV
Mikiya Kobayashi
Plastic
H: 60cm (23in)
W: 28cm (11in)
D: 16cm (6¼in)
Mikiya Kobayashi,
Japan
www.mikiyakobayashi.com

(right)
**Table for
children, Eva**
Lawrence and
Sharon Tarantino
Foam
H: 44.5cm (17½in)
W: 55cm (21½in)
D: 71cm (28in)
Offi, US
www.offi.com

(right)
**Micro pavilion,
Concrete-pod**
Kazuya Morita
Fibre-reinforced
concrete
H: 170cm (66in)
Diam: 170cm (66in)
Kazuya Morita
Architecture Studio,
Japan
www.morita-arch.com

(left)
Nest/cave, Nido
Javier Mariscal
Rotation-moulded
polyethylene
H: 83cm (32in)
W: 104cm (41in)
L: 150cm (59in)
Magis SpA, Italy
www.magismetoo.com

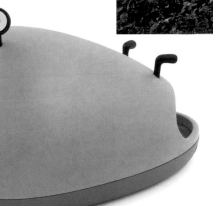

(above)
**Children's seat,
Mini Tumbly**
Annet Neugebauer
Polyethylene
H: 38cm (15in)
W: 25.5cm (10¼in)
D: 36cm (14⅛in)
De Vorm, the
Netherlands
www.devorm.nl

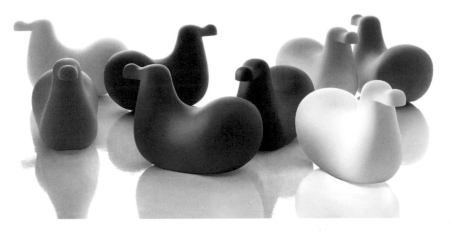

(left)
Rocking bird, Dodo
Oiva Toikka
Rotation-moulded
polyethylene
H: 58.5cm (23in)
W: 41.5cm (16½in)
L: 86cm (33in)
Magis SpA, Italy
www.magisdesign.com

(right)
**Ride-on vehicle,
Sibis Max**
Wolfgang Sirch and
Christoph Bitzer
Steam-bent ash wood
H: 37cm (14⅝in)
H (seat): 23cm (9in)
W: 25cm (9⅞in)
L: 57cm (22in)
Sirch Holzverarbeitung,
Germany
www.sirch.de

(above)
Trailer, Sibis Lorette
Wolfgang Sirch and
Christoph Bitzer
Birch plywood
H: 32cm (12⅝in)
W: 33cm (13in)
L: 44cm (17⅜in)
Sirch Holzverarbeitung,
Germany
www.sirch.de

(above)
**Wheelbarrow
for children
(with tiltable tray),**
Franz Sirch
Laminated birch
plywood
H: 42.5cm (16⁷/₈in)
W: 48.5cm (19¹/₄in)
L: 57cm (22in)
Sirch, Germany
www.sirch.de

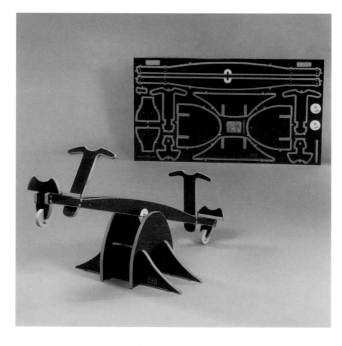

(above)
**Wheelbarrow
(puzzle furniture),
Bene**
Jörn Alexander Stelzner
Plywood with a birch
veneer, coated with
coloured phenol resin
H: 40cm (15¾in)
W: 32cm (12⅝in)
L: 53cm (20in)
Tau, Germany
www.tau.de

(left)
**Puzzle furniture,
Seesaw**
Jörn Alexander Stelzner
Plywood with a birch
veneer, coated with
coloured phenol resin
H: 68cm (26in)
W: 60cm (23in)
L: 146cm (57in)
Tau, Germany
www.tau.de

(left)
**Cardboard igloo,
The Paperpod**
Paul Martin
Cardboard
H: 125cm (49in)
W: 150cm (59in)
D: 150cm (59in)
Paperpod Cardboard
Creations Ltd, UK
www.paperpod.co.uk

(above)
**Play shed, Modern
Playshed**
Ryan Grey Smith
Exterior-grade fir
plywood, plexiglass
H: 193cm (76in)
W: 224cm (88in)
D: 112cm (44in)
Modern-Shed, US
www.modern-shed.com

(above)
**Customized
playhouse, Qb**
Claudia Keijzers
Wood
H: 125cm (49in)
W: 250cm (98in)
D: 150cm (59in)
qb, Choose Build Play!,
the Netherlands
www.quubi.com

(right)
**Soapbox cart,
Play Soapbox Cart**
Jesper K. Thomsen
Varnished beech
H: 38cm (15in)
W: 70cm (27in)
D: 123cm (48in)
Normann Copenhagen,
Denmark
www.normann
copenhagen.com

(right)
Tree house, Parody II,
Sanei Hopkins
Architects
Corrugated
galvanized steel
L: 300cm (118in)
Diam: 150cm (59in)
Sanei Hopkins
Architects, UK
www.saneihopkins.co.uk

(facing page)
Playscape, Four x 4
Nocturnal Design Lab
Cedar timber,
galvanized metal
H: 11.5–488cm
(4½–192in)
W: 11.5–366cm
(4½–144in)
D: 11.5–366cm
(4½–144in)
Nocturnal
Design Lab, US
www.nocturnal
designlab.com

(above)
**Children's playhouse,
Dreaming Spires
Willow Playhouse**
Judith Needham
Willow, FSC-certified
pine, kite fabric
H: 200cm (78in)
W: 240cm (94in)
D: 100cm (39in)
Judith Needham, UK
www.judithneedham.co.uk

(right)
Play house, Parody I
Sanei Hopkins
Architects
Timber, glass,
corrugated
galvanized steel
H: 180cm (70in)
W: 180cm (70in)
D: 240cm (94in)
Sanei Hopkins
Architects, UK
www.saneihopkins.co.uk

(right)
**Garden gnomes,
Set of 3 (Werner,
Heinz and Martin)**
Formanek.ch
Powder-coated steel
H: 14cm (5½in)
Pulpo, Germany
www.pulpoproducts.com

(left)
**Tote Bag, Picnica
Tote Bag by
Eding:Post**
Tomohiro Kato, Satoshi
Hasegawa
Nylon
H (when collapsed):
25cm (9⅞in)
H (when opened):
30cm (11¾in)
W (when collapsed):
15cm (5⅞in)
W (when opened):
33cm (13in)
D (when collapsed):
10.5cm (4⅛in)
D (when opened):
9mm (⅜in)
Greener Grass
Design, US
www.greeener
grassdesign.com

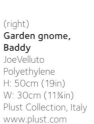

(left)
Stool, Tea Cup Stool
Holly Palmer
Rotation-moulded
MDPE plastic
H: 41cm (16⅛in)
Diam: 58cm (22in)
Mocha, UK
www.mocha.uk.com

(right)
**Garden gnome,
Baddy**
JoeVelluto
Polyethylene
H: 50cm (19in)
W: 30cm (11¾in)
Plust Collection, Italy
www.plust.com

(above)
Stool, Pello
Erik Österlund
Zinc-plated and
galvanized steel
H: 50cm (19in)
Diam: 41cm
(16⅛in)
Nola, Sweden
www.nola.se

(above)
**Meeting shelter,
Leaf Shelter**
Superblue Design Ltd
Glowing edge
UV-resistant acrylic,
mild steel, zinc and
polyester powder-
coated, stainless
steel fixings
H: 240cm (94in)
Diam: 180cm (70in)
Superblue
Design Ltd, UK
www.superblue.co.uk

(left)
**Trunk/container,
El Baúl**
Javier Mariscal
Rotation-moulded
polyethylene
H: 56cm (22in)
W: 91cm (35in)
D: 61cm (24in)
Magis SpA, Italy
www.magismetoo.com

(above)
**Gym and relaxation
wellness cushion,
Waff® Max**
Andy Tomarc
PVC
H: 45cm (17¾in)
Diam: 145cm (57in)
Waff, France
www.waffweb.com

(right)
**Low chair, bench and
low table, Piedras**
Javier Mariscal
Rotation-moulded
polyethylene
H (chair and bench):
47cm (18½in)
H (table):
25cm (9⅞in)
L (bench):
117.5cm (46in)
D: 60cm (23in)
Magis SpA, Italy
www.magisdesign.com

(below)
**Seating, Flying
Carpet**
Eeno Aarnio
Rotation-moulded
polyethylene,
polyamide
H: 28cm (11in)
W: 100cm (39in)
L: 120cm (47in)
Magis SpA, Italy
www.magisdesign.com

(above)
Armchair, Mia
Rachel and Benoit
Convers
Printed
polypropylene, steel
H: 60cm (23in)
W: 90cm (35in)
D: 70cm (27in)
Ibride, France
www.ibride.fr

(left)
Light, BMWV
Moonlight
Polyethylene
Battery-operated lamp
Diam: 35, 55 or 75cm
(13¾, 21 or 29in)
Moonlight GmbH,
Germany
www.moonlight.info

(above)
Outdoor wireless speakers, AQ Wireless Outdoor Speakers
AQ
Plastic
H: 20cm (7⅞in)
W: 6cm (2⅜in)
AQ Speakers, UK
www.aqsound.com

(left)
Floating wireless speaker, Aqua Sounders
Grace Digital
Plastic
Diam: 16.5cm
(6½in)
Grace Digital, US
www.gracedigitalaudio.com

(above)
Portable waterproof speaker, Drop
Dreams Inc.
Plastic
H: 22.5cm (9in)
Diam: 16.5cm
(6½in)
Zumreed, Japan
www.zumreed.net

(right)
Wireless outdoor speaker, Freewheeler
Ron Arad, Francesco Pellisari
Lacquered wood
W: 25cm (9⅞in)
Diam: 58cm (22in)
Viteo Outdoors, Austria
www.viteo.at

(left)
**Outdoor lamp
with incorporated
speaker, Ibiza**
Francesco Rota
Polyethylene,
stainless steel
1 x max 20W-E27
H: 70 or 120cm
(27 or 47in)
W: 12cm (4¾in)
Oluce srl, Italy
www.oluce.com

(above)
Speaker, Zemi
E. Frolet, F. Pellisari
Glazed ceramic
H (without cable):
23cm (9in)
Diam: 26 cm (10¼in)
Viteo Outdoors, Austria
www.viteo.at

(above)
**Environmental
speaker, Bose
FreeSpace® 51
Environmental
Speaker**
Bose
Plastic
H: 38cm (15in)
W: 37cm (14⅝in)
Bose, US
www.bose.co.uk

(right)
**Speaker, Outdoor
Weatherproof
Speakers, PAN-SPKB**
Joe Pantel
Polygraphite
H: 28cm (11in)
W: 24cm (9½in)
D: 19cm (7½in)
Pantel Corp, US
www.panteltv.com

(left)
Movie screen,
Open Air Pro Screen
Open Air Cinema
Inflatable frame
H (projection surface):
152cm (60in)
W (projection surface):
274cm (108in)
Open Air Cinema, US
www.openaircinema.us

(above)
Wireless outdoor
speaker system,
OutCast
Soundcast Systems
High-impact plastic
with weatherproof
electronics
H: 66cm (26in)
Diam (bottom):
28cm (11in)
Soundcast Systems, US
wwwsoundcastsystems.com

(left)
Backyard Outdoor
Theatre System
Frontgate
Aluminium frame
H: 274cm (108in)
W: 366cm (144in)
Frontgate, US
www.frontgate.com

(above)
**All-weather outdoor
LCD TV, 3230HD**
SunBriteTV
All-weather outdoor
rated ASA plastic resin
H: 56cm (22in)
W: 82cm (32in)
D: 15cm (6in)
SunBriteTV, US
www.sunbritetv.com

(above)
**All-weather outdoor
HDTV, PAN321**
Joe Pantel
Aluminium housing with
internal temperature
control system
H: 65cm (25in)
W (screen diagonal
measure): 81cm (32in)
L: 85cm (33in)
Pantel Corp, US
www.panteltv.com

(right)
**All-weather outdoor
LCD TV, 5510HD**
SunBriteTV
Powder-coated
aluminium
H: 84cm (33in)
W: 133cm (52in)
D: 20cm (8in)
SunBriteTV, US
www.sunbritetv.com

(facing page)
**All-weather outdoor
LCD HDTV, 47"**
AQUiVO
Glass, LCD panel,
aluminium
H: 112.3cm (44in)
W: 66.7cm (26in)
D: 12cm (4¾in)
Aquivo, UK
www.ciao.co.uk

Cooking and heating

(right)
Alfresco dining table, Spray Stone Plancha Table
Red Hot Plancha Company
Resin composite
H: 72cm (28in)
Diam: 93–180cm (36in–70in)
The Red Hot Plancha Company, UK
www.redhotplancha.com

(above)
Cooking table, Menes
Alpina
Stainless steel, wood
H: 72.9cm (28in)
L: 236.3cm (93in)
D: 96.3cm (37in)
Alpina, Belgium
www.alpina-grills.be

(left)
Table, TepanGrill Table
Troy Adams
Honed, absolute black granite, stainless steel
H: 76cm (30in)
W: 122cm (48in)
L: 122cm (48in)
Troy Adams Design, US
www.troyadamsdesign.com

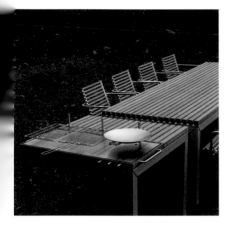

(above)
**Table with barbecue,
ExTempore
Barbecue Table**
Arnold Merckx
Jatoba wood,
aluminium,
stainless steel
H: 75cm (29in)
W: 90cm (35in)
D: 90cm (35in)
Extremis, Belgium
www.extremis.be

(above)
**Kitchen table,
Cucina Pontile**
Jacques Toussaint
Stainless steel
structure, iroko
wood slats
H: 83cm (32in)
L: 160cm (63in)
D: 80cm (31in)
Dimensione
Disegno srl, Italy
www.
dimensionedisegno.it

(left)
**Cooking table
with barbecue,
Las Brisas 92**
Talocci Design
Laminam,
stainless steel
H: 92–97cm
(36–38in)
L: 142cm (56in)
D: 70cm (27in)
Foppa Pedretti
SpA, Italy
www.foppapedretti.it

(right)
**Customizable
outdoor kitchen,
Fuego Modular**
Robert Brunner
Slate, teak, cast iron,
stainless steel
H: 110cm (43¼in)
W: 265cm (104¼in)
D: 127cm (50in)
Fuego North
America, US
www.fuegoliving.com

(above)
**Table barbecue,
Table BBQ/Heat Range**
Henrik Pedersen
Stainless steel, steel
H: 20cm (7⅞in)
W: 30cm (11¾in)
L: 60cm (23in)
Design House
Denmark, Denmark
www.designhouse
denmark.dk

(left)
**Kitchen, Outdoor
Kitchen Sink,
Outdoor Kitchen
Table 62, Outdoor
Kitchen BBQ**
Wolfgang Pichler
Stainless steel, teak
H: 76cm (29in)
W: 62cm (24in)
L: 270cm (106in)
Viteo Outdoors, Austria
www.viteo.at

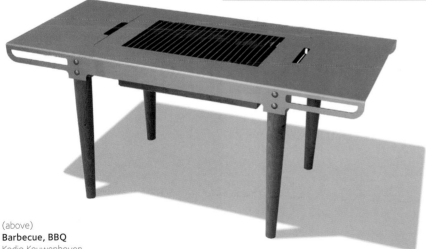

(above)
**Social cooking
appliances, Affinity
30G Cooktop**
Bob Shingler
Stainless steel
Diam: 76cm (30in)
Evo, Inc, US
www.evoamerica.com.

(above)
**Barbecue,
Echelon 1060i**
R.H. Peterson
Stainless steel
H (from work surface):
37cm (14⅝in)
W: 127cm (50in)
D: 61cm (24in)
R.H. Peterson, US
www.fire-magic.co.uk

(right)
**Outdoor Kitchen,
Kingston 2008**
R.H. Peterson
Stainless steel,
teak and slate
H to work surface:
95cm (37in)
Barbecue hood:
37cm (14⅝in)
W: 300cm (118in)
D: 75cm (29in)
The Lapa Company &
R.H. Peterson, UK & US
www.fire-magic.co.uk

(above)
**Kitchen, Luxius nr. 1
Outdoor Kitchen**
Newtrend
Natural oak,
stainless steel, granite,
Boretti Black Mezzo
Top stove
H: 90cm (35in)
W: 217.5cm (86in)
Luxius Outdoor
Kitchens, the
Netherlands
www.luxius.nl

(above)
**Barbecue,
Aurora A540i**
RH Peterson
Stainless Steel
H (from work surface):
37cm (14⅝in)
W: 81cm (31in)
D: 50cm (19in)
R.H. Peterson, US
www.fire-magic.co.uk

(right)
**Barbecue, Electrolux
Jeppe Utzon BBQ**
Jeppe Utzon
Corian®, stainless steel
H: 80cm (31in)
L: 156cm (61in)
D: 66.2cm (26in)
Electrolux, Australia
www.electrolux.com.au

Wolfgang Pichler

There is no better illustration of our changing relationship with indoors and outdoors than the kitchen. In the last decade, attitudes to eating alfresco, in northern Europe especially, have changed dramatically. Climate change for some of us means we can now live as those in Mediterranean climates have lived for eons. Eating outside has absorbed the interest of a number of innovative product and industrial designers and Viteo Outdoors, a company that specializes in outdoor furniture and accessories, is at the forefront of the interface between interior and exterior design. Wolfgang Pichler is the artistic and intellectual mastermind behind this Austrian company, where there is a real accent on materials and craft skills, and where products are made in association with local craftsmen.

Pichler initially trained as an architect and founded Viteo Outdoors in 2001. "I was trying to buy outdoor furniture for our home," he says, "but couldn't find anything I liked so I decided to make it myself. To begin with, interior elements were put outside, then different new materials were found and the indoor-outdoor concepts started to break through. It was new territory for furniture companies and it was a really fast growing market. Personally," he continues, "I had always been very attracted to the outdoors and I've always felt there should be a complementary relationship between indoor and outdoor space, that there should be a flow between them. This is what I try to realize in my architectural projects."

Outdoor cooking is no longer limited to barbecues. You can now transport the whole kitchen, complete with fridges, sinks, cupboards and state-of-the-art work surfaces and appliances, down the garden. So now you can prepare as well as cook your gourmet meal outside. The Viteo Outdoors Kitchen designed by Pichler is a modular system, which gives you the opportunity to customize your kitchen to suit your culinary desires – it includes a barbecue, teppanyaki grill, sink and wide work surfaces. "We all like to be outside," says Pichler. "Spending time outdoors is important for everybody and the idea of doing something you would typically do indoors, like cooking in an outdoor area, is really thrilling. As far as the design is concerned, it's almost the same as an indoor kitchen – except with influences like sun, rain, dust and wind, you have to find the right materials and fittings. The way we cook outdoors is, however, quite different to the way we cook indoors – good design, in this case," he says, "is understanding how we use our outdoor kitchens."

The latest edition to Viteo's outdoor heating and cooking range is the new Cementum Collection (*see* p.351), made in collaboration with Austrian designer Gerd Rosenauer and the manufacturer Concreto. This is also a modular system, which includes products for heating, cooking and seating, but with pared-down form and strong, sculptual qualities it is made of a far less predictable material – concrete. As an architect, Pichler says he has a natural affinity for cement, praising its "authenticity and honesty and the way over time it develops a rich patina".

The Cementum Collection is designed for relaxed lounging, it's the campfire concept, though ultra-modern in design, reduced to the bare essentials. "The idea for the collection," says Pichler, "started with simplicity of materials and design – something elemental like fire in combination with purist design was something new. While the idea of sitting around a campfire is something very primeval and appealing to us all." The campfire idea is a popular theme at present. Extremis make a huge fire bowl called Qrater, while Tulp offer Lotus (*see* p351).

What would Pichler say defines the Viteo design aesthetic? "Nature," he replies, "a straight line is not something alien to nature." Even a blossom has geometric elements. "Every item we design," says Pichler, "has to follow the Viteo philosophy; honesty, restraint and truth to materials. I personally always try to find logical and understandable elements with my designs."

(left)
Outdoor kitchen, Kitchen XL/Home Collection
Wolfgang Pichler
Stainless steel
H: 95cm (37in)
H (with the sink): 115cm (45in)
L: 139cm (55in)
Viteo Outdoors, Austria
www.viteo.at

(above)
**Sink cabinet, Splash
Sink Cabinet**
Mark Suensilpong
Teak, stainless steel
H: 85cm (33in)
W: 160cm (63in)
D: 60cm (24in)
Jane Hamley Wells, US
www.janehamleywells.com

(above)
**Barbecue, 4-Burner
Barbecue Heat Range**
Henrik Pedersen
Stainless steel
H: 82.5cm (32in)
W: 50cm (19in)
L: 100cm (39in)
Design House Denmark,
Denmark
www.designhouse
denmark.dk

(right)
**Outdoor Bar and
Margarita Centre**
Twin Eagles
Stainless steel
W (outdoor bar):
72cm (28½in)
D (outdoor bar):
25cm (10in)
W (margarita centre):
42cm (16½in)
D (margarita centre):
25cm (10in)
Twin Eagles, US
www.twineaglesinc.com

(left)
Outdoor freezer drawers, 24" Outdoor Freezer Drawers
Kalamazoo Outdoor Gourmet
Stainless steel
H: 86cm (34in)
W: 61cm (24in)
D:61cm (24in)
Kalamazoo Outdoor Gourmet, US
www.kalamazoogourmet.com

(above)
Outdoor refrigerator, 48" Outdoor Glass-Door Refrigerator and Refrigerated Drawers
Kalamazoo Outdoor Gourmet
Stainless steel, glass
H: 86cm (34in)
W: 122cm (48in)
D: 61cm (24in)
Kalamazoo Outdoor Gourmet, US
www.kalamazoogourmet.com

(right)
Outdoor wine chiller, 24" Wine Chiller
Kalamazoo Outdoor Gourmet
Stainless steel, glass
H: 87cm (34¼in)
W: 61cm (24in)
D: 61cm (24in)
Kalamazoo Outdoor Gourmet, US
www.kalamazoogourmet.com

(left)
**Outdoor keg
tapper, 24" Outdoor
Keg Tapper**
Kalamazoo
Outdoor Gourmet
Stainless steel
H (cabinet):
86cm (34in)
W: 61cm (24in)
D: 61cm (24in)
Kalamazoo Outdoor
Gourmet, US
www.kalamazoo
gourmet.com

(above)
**Refrigerator/Beer
dispenser, 48" Keg
Tapper and Glass
Door Refrigerator**
Kalamazoo Outdoor
Gourmet
Stainless steel
H: 86cm (34in)
L: 122cm (48in)
D: 61cm (24in)
Kalamazoo Outdoor
Gourmet, US
www.kalamazoo
gourmet.com

(right)
Outdoor refrigerator
Twin Eagles
Stainless steel
H: 88cm (34½in)
W: 62cm (24½in)
Twin Eagles, US
www.twineaglesbbq.com

(above)
**Outdoor Island
Grill, 9000X**
Electrolux
Stainless steel,
teak wood
H: 99cm (39in)
W: 160cm (63in)
D: 89cm (35in)
Electrolux, Italy
www.electrolux.co.uk

(above)
**Gas barbecue,
Diamento™**
Pininfarina
Steel
H: 112cm (44in)
L (maximum):
210.5cm (82in)
D: 73.5cm (29in)
Coleman, Italy
www.coleman.eu

(right)
**Grilling centre,
Grillzebo™**
Metal, fibre stone
LED lights
H: 231cm (91in)
W: 262cm (103in)
L: 152cm (60in)
Brookstone, US
www.brookstone.com

(left)
**Mobile cooking unit,
Bongos BG002**
Alpina
Stainless steel
H: 103cm (41in)
W: 77.5cm (30in)
L: 174cm (68in)
Alpina, Belgium
www.alpina-grills.be

(above)
Kitchen, Suzette
Alpina
Stainless steel, wood
H: 85cm (33in)
L: 147.4cm (58in)
D: 66.5cm (26in)
Alpina, Belgium
www.alpina-grills.be

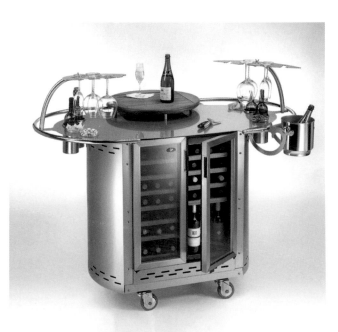

(left)
**Mobile cocktail bar,
Bongos Drink**
Alpina
Stainless steel
H: 112cm (44in)
W: 84cm (33in)
L: 141cm (56in)
Alpina, Belgium
www.alpina-grills.be

(left)
**Mobile wine cellar,
Bongos Wine**
Alpina
Stainless steel, glass
H: 111cm (44in)
W: 159cm (63in)
D: 106cm (42in)
Alpina, Belgium
www.alpina-grills.be

(above)
**Outdoor electric grill,
Fuego 02 Electric**
Robert Brunner
Slate, teak, cast iron,
stainless steel
H: 93cm (36½in)
W: 70cm (27½in)
D: 83cm (32½in)
Fuego North
America, US
www.fuegoliving.com

(above)
**Outdoor grill,
Fuego 01**
Robert Brunner
Slate, teak, cast iron,
stainless steel
H: 90cm (35¼in)
W: 91cm (35½in)
D: 101cm (39⅝in)
Fuego North
America, US
www.fuegoliving.com

(right)
Outdoor grill, T-Grill
Grand Hall
Steel, stainless steel
H: 117cm (46in)
W: 114cm (45in)
D: 71cm (28in)
Grand Hall, the
Netherlands
www.grandhall.eu

(above and left)
Free-standing grill, Edo Grill
Kalamazoo Outdoor Gourmet
Stainless steel
H: 97cm (38¼in)
W: 123cm (48½in)
W (open):
200cm (78in)
D: 80cm (31½in)
Kalamazoo Outdoor Gourmet, US
www.kalamazoo gourmet.com

(right)
Outdoor grill, Grill Stainless
Ralph Kraeuter
Stainless steel
H: 89cm (35in)
W: 87cm (34in)
D: 51cm (20in)
Radius Design, Germany
www.radius-design.com

(right)
Barbecue,
Dancook 1800
Dancook
Stainless steel
Diam: 58cm (22in)
Dancook, Denmark
www.dancook.dk

(above)
Barbecue, BBQ02
Stefano Gallizioli
Satin stainless
steel, Corian®
H: 112cm (44in)
W: 61cm (24in)
L: 112cm (44in)
Coro, Italy
www.coroitalia.it

(above)
Bonfire,
Dancook 9000
Dancook
Stainless steel
H: 50cm (19in)
W: 71.5cm (28in)
D: 71.5cm (28in)
Dancook, Denmark
www.dancook.dk

(right)
Barbecue
and kitchen,
Dancook Kitchen
Dancook
Granite, stainless
steel, aluminium
W (table top):
62cm (24in)
L (table top):
62cm (24in)
Diam (barbecue):
58cm (22in)
Dancook, Denmark
www.dancook.dk

(above)
**Outdoor grill,
Element Grill**
Robert Brunner
Stainless steel,
golden leaf chestnut
wood, cast iron
H: 92cm (36in)
W: 69cm (27in)
D: 69cm (27in)
Element by Fuego, US
www.elementby
fuego.com

(above)
**Barbecue,
Tondo Maxi**
Marco Ferreri
Stainless steel
H: 101cm (40in)
Diam: 55cm (21in)
Dimensione Disegno
srl, Italy
www.dimensione
disegno.it

(left)
Flat-top grill, Evo
Alpina
Steel
Diam: 76.2cm (29in)
Alpina, Belgium
www.alpina-grills.be

(above)
Grill, Blitzgrill
Ralph Kraeuter
Stainless steel, cast iron
H: 86.5cm (34in)
W: 38cm (15in)
D: 56cm (22in)
Radius Design,
Germany
www.radius-design.com

(above)
**Portable gas grill,
CityBoy Picnic Grill**
Klaus Aalto
Steel, stainless steel,
oak, Primus gas burner
H: 22cm (8⅝in)
W: 18cm (7⅛in)
D: 18cm (7⅛in)
Selki-Asema, Finland
www.selki-asema.fi

(above)
**Gas barbecue,
Alessi Barbicù**
Piero Lissoni
Painted steel,
stainless steel
H: 38.5cm (15⅜in)
W: 40cm (15¾in)
L: 69.5cm (27in)
Alessi with
Fochista, Italy
www.alessi.com

(left)
Barbecue, Taurus
Michael Sieger
Steel
H: 99cm (39in)
W: 95cm (37in)
D: 48cm (18⅞in)
Conmoto, Germany
www.conmoto.com

(left and below)
Modular barbecue trolley, Alessi Barbicù
Piero Lissoni
Painted steel, thermoplastic resin
H (vertically): 81.5cm (32in)
H (horizontally): 46cm (18⅛in)
W (vertically): 44.5cm (17¾in)
W (horizontally): 75.5cm (29in)
L (vertically): 79cm (31in)
L (horizontally): 80.5cm (32in)
Alessi with Fochista, Italy
www.alessi.com

(above)
Barbecue, Hotwater Barbecue
Marco Sangiorgi
Stainless steel, wood
H: 79cm (31in)
W: 75cm (29in)
L: 130cm (51in)
Beltempo, Peru
www.beltempo.org

(left)
Barbecue, TPL BBQ
Sante Martinuzzi
Stainless steel
H (closed): 91cm (35in)
H (open): 87cm (34in)
W: 56.8cm (22in)
L (closed): 72cm (28in)
L (open): 144.5cm (57in)
TPL srl, Italy
www.teakparkline.it

(left)
Barbecue, Quadro
Adalberto Mestre
Painted steel
H: 120cm (47in)
L: 50cm (19in)
D: 50cm (19in)
Dimensione Disegno srl, Italy
www.dimensione disegno.it

(right)
**Gas grill,
Gastronomical
(Eva Solo)**
Tools, Henrik Holbaek
and Claus Jensen
Stainless steel
H: 80cm (31in)
Diam: 60cm (23in)
Eva Denmark
A/S, Denmark
www.evadenmark.com

(above)
**Table grill, To Go
(Eva Solo)**
Tools, Henrik Holbaek
and Claus Jensen
Porcelain,
stainless steel
H: 20cm (7⅞in)
Diam: 31cm
(12¼in)
Eva Denmark
A/S, Denmark
www.evadenmark.com

(above)
Fireplace, Magic
Fried Ulber
Stainless steel
H: 57cm (22in)
W: 40cm (15¾in)
D: 34cm (13⅜in)
Conmoto, Germany
www.conmoto.com

(left)
**Fire tray/grill,
Langgrill**
Möbel-Liebschaften
Oxidized steel
H: 25cm (9⅞in)
W: 45cm (17¾in)
L: 95cm (37in)
Möbel-Liebschaften,
Germany
www.moebel-
liebschaften.de

(left)
**Pizza oven, Outdoor
Artisan Pizza Oven**
Kalamazoo Outdoor
Gourmet
Stainless steel,
composite baking stone
H: 45cm (17¾in)
W: 74cm (29¼in)
D: 75cm (29½in)
Kalamazoo Outdoor
Gourmet, US
www.kalamazoo
gourmet.com

(above)
**Barbecue for outdoor
fireplace, Bon-fire**
René Stage,
Torben Eriksen
Steel
H. 140cm (55in)
Diam: 70cm (27in)
Bon-fire, Denmark
www.bon-fire.dk

(left)
**Wood pellet grill,
Lil' Pig (BBQPIG)**
Joseph P/ Traeger
Steel
H: 115cm (45in)
W: 77cm (30½in)
L: 122cm (48in)
Traeger Pellet Grills
LLC, US
www.traegergrills.com

(above)
**Barbecue,
Weber® Q™200**
Weber
Cast aluminium,
enamelled cast iron,
glass-reinforced nylon
frame, stainless steel
H: 66.1cm (26in)
W: 80.5cm-130.6cm
(31in-51in)
D: 61.8cm (24in)
Weber, US
www.weber.com

(left)
Fireplace, Gryll
Wodkte
Pre-treated,
rusted steel
H: 133.8cm (53in)
W: 47cm (18½in)
D: 47cm (18½in)
Wodkte GmbH,
Germany
www.wodtke.com

(right)
**Firewood trolley,
Kaminholzwagen**
Michael Rösing,
Michael Schuster
Steel
H: 110cm (43in)
W: 41cm (16⅛in)
L: 41cm (16⅛in)
Radius Design, Germany
www.radius-design.com

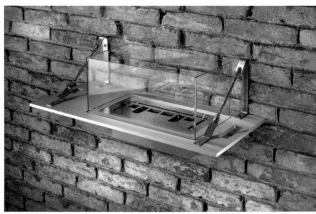

(above)
**Fireplace,
G.Flame Wall**
Giulio Gianturco
Aluminium, stainless
steel, glass ceramic
Schott®
H: 22cm (8⅝in)
L: 78cm (30in)
D: 35cm (13¾in)
Dimensione
Disegno srl, Italy
www.dimensione
disegno.it

(left)
Balcony grill, Bruce
Henrik Johannes Drecker
Steel
H: 20cm (7⅞in)
W: 22cm (8⅝in)
L: 65cm (25in)
Astor Wohnideen,
Germany
www.design-3000.de
www.astor-wohnideen.de

(above)
**Table, Cementum
Firetable 140**
Wolfgang Pichler
Concrete
H: 20cm (7⅞in)
W: 103cm (41in)
L: 140cm (55in)
Viteo Outdoors, Austria
www.viteo.at

(above)
Fire bowl, Lotus
Roderick Vos
Cast aluminium
H: 76cm (29in)
Diam: 105cm (34⅜in)
Tulp, the Netherlands
www.tulp.eu

(left)
Fire dish, Qrater
Dirk Wynants
Weathering steel
H: 25cm (9⅞in)
Diam: 145cm (57in)
Extremis, Belgium
www.extremis.be

(above)
**Fire feature,
Lotus Bowl**
Elena Colombo
Stainless steel
Diam: 122cm (48in)
Colombo Construction
Corp., US
www.firefeatures.com

(above)
Fireplace, Gollnick
Carsten Gollnick
Painted steel,
stainless steel
H: 29cm (11⅜in)
Diam (outer):
69cm (27in)
Conmoto, Germany
www.conmoto.com

(right)
**Fire feature,
Square Dish**
Elena Colombo
Stainless steel
W: 152cm (60in)
L: 152cm (60in)
Colombo Construction
Corp., US
www.firefeatures.com

(above)
Fire basket, Terra
Ralph Kondermann
Stainless steel
H: 30cm (11¾in)
Diam: 42cm (16½in)
Blomus GmbH,
Germany
www.blomus.com

(right)
Torch cage, Glow
Eva Schildt
Powder-coated
aluminium
H: 54 or 124cm
(21 or 49in)
Diam: 51cm (20in)
Flora Wilh. Förster
GmbH & Co. KG,
Germany
www.flora-online.de

(above)
Fire basket, Baron
Röshults
Iron
H: 105cm (41in)
Diam: 50cm (19in)
Röshults, Sweden
www.roshults.se

(left)
Fireplace, Fera
Sebastian David
Büscher
Stainless steel
H: 26cm (10¼in)
Diam: 46cm (18⅛in)
Conmoto, Germany
www.conmoto.com

**Fire sculpture,
Firepit**
Cathy Azria
Steel
W (wigwam fire):
40cm (15¾in)
W (fire pit):
55cm (21in)
L (wigwam fire):
65cm (25in)
L (fire pit):
100cm (39in)
BDesign, UK
www.bd-designs.co.uk

(above)
Fire sculpture, Planes
Cathy Azria
Steel
H: 75cm (29in)
Diam: 70cm (27in)
BDesign, UK
www.bd-designs.co.uk

(right)
Fireplace, Zero
Matteo Galbusera
Ivano Losa,
Steel
H: 40cm (15¾in)
Diam: 145cm (57in)
Ak47, Italy
www.ak47space.com

(below)
Portable fireplace,
EcoSmart Fire Cyl
The Fire Company
Stainless steel,
toughened glass
H: 53.3cm (20in)
Diam: 44cm (17⅜in)
The Fire Company,
Australia
www.ecosmartfire.com

(above)
Fire feature,
Branchwall
Elena Colombo
Stainless steel
H: 274cm (108in)
W: 244cm (96in)
Colombo Construction
Corp., US
www.firefeatures.com

(left)
Floor fire, Takibi
Michael Koenig
Powder-coated steel
H: 119cm (47in)
W: 28cm (11in)
L: 67cm (26in)
Artepuro, Germany
www.artepuro.de

(left)
**Fireplace and
seating, Dots**
Studio Aisslinger
Steel, glass, fabric
H (Fire Dot):
64cm (25in)
H (Sit Dot):
43cm (16⅞in)
Diam (Fire Dot):
45cm (17¾in)
Diam (Sit Dot small):
40cm (15¾in)
Diam (Sit Dot large):
70cm (27in)
Conmoto, Germany
www.conmoto.com

(above)
Fireplace, Cubico XT
Jan des Bouvrie
Stainless steel
H: 123.5cm (49in)
W: 70cm (27in)
D: 20cm (7⅞in)
Safretti BV, the
Netherlands
www.safretti.com

(above)
Fireplace, Curva
Jan des Bouvrie
Powder-coated steel
H: 70cm (27in)
W: 70cm (27in)
D: 17.5cm (6⅞in)
Safretti BV,
the Netherlands
www.safretti.com

(right)
Fire, Jar
Christophe Pillet
Concrete, glass
H: 77.1cm (30in)
Diam: 41cm (16⅛in)
Planika, Poland
www.planikafires.com

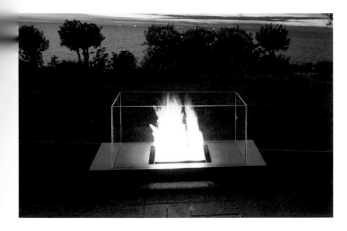

(left)
Fireplace, Uni Flame
Radius Design
Steel
H: 46cm (18⅛in)
W: 40cm (15¾in)
L: 99cm (39in)
Radius Design, Germany
www.radius-design.com

(below)
Mobile fireplace,
Travelmate
Studio Vertijet
Powder-coated steel,
stainless steel, glass,
ceramics
H: 50cm (19in)
W: 70cm (27in)
D: 20cm (7⅞in)
Conmoto, Germany
www.conmoto.com

(above)
Fire feature,
Fire Rings
Elena Colombo
Corten steel
Diam: 61–183cm
(24–72in)
Colombo Construction
Corp., US
www.firefeatures.com

(right)
Fireplace, urBonfire
Michael Hilgers
Polished stainless steel,
borosilicate glass
H: 47cm (18½in)
Diam: 47cm (18⅓in)
Rephorm, Germany
www.rephorm.de

(above)
Firebox, Quadro
Conmoto
Black varnished
steel, stainless steel
H: 16cm (6¼in)
W: 34cm (13⅜in)
D: 21cm (8¼in)
Conmoto, Germany
www.conmoto.com

(above)
**Fire feature,
Branch Trough**
Elena Colombo
Stainless steel
L: 244cm (96in)
Colombo Construction
Corp., US
www.firefeatures.com

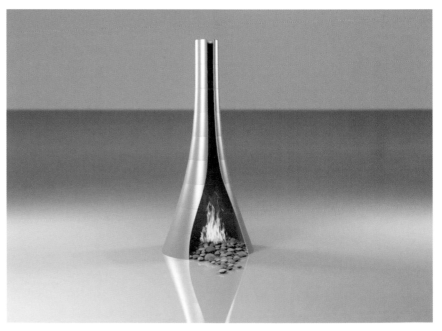

(right)
**Fire feature,
Fire stack**
Elena Colombo
Stainless steel
H: 274cm (108in)
Colombo Construction
Corp., US
www.firefeatures.com

The publisher would like to thank the designers, the manufacturers and the following photographers for the use of their material.

10-11: Joost van Brug
12 bottom: Mia Serra
13 bottom: © Adam Booth
14 top: Simon Devitt
25 top: Joost van Brug
28 top: Andy Sturgeon
42 top: James Hacker
66 top: Gerard van Hees
82 bottom right: Gianluca Ruocco Guadagno
88 middle right: Morgane Le Gall
92 middle: Morgane Le Gall
101 top: Steve Gunther
102 top: © Charlotte Rowe Garden Design
108 top: John Ellis
108 bottom: JD Petersen
109 top: Murray Fredericks
110 top: Dean Bradley
111 top left: Patrick Redmond
111 top right: Patrick Redmond
121 top: © Kenkoon
126 top: Shane Kohatsu
131 top right: Helen PE
146 top: Rene van der Hulst
147 top: Steve Speller
149 top: photographed by Liesa Cole and Tony Rodio of Omni Studios, styled by Chatham Hellmers
152 bottom: Ingmar Cramers
179 bottom: David Levin
182 top: Erich Wimberger
182 bottom: EGO Paris-A. Chideric-Studio Kalice-www.kalice.fr
183 top and middle: Variant srl
185 bottom: Sandro Paderni
196 middle: © Kenkoon
202 top: Studiopiù Communication srl, emupress@studiopiu.org
205 middle: Alessandro Paderni
209 middle: Marc Eggimann © Vitra 2009
213 middle right: Paul Tahon and Ronan & Erwan Bouroullec © Vitra
225 bottom: John Curry
228 middle: Sandro Paderni
233: Jäger & Jäger
234 top: Anice

Hoachlander
237: George Logan
238 top right: Jäger & Jäger
240 middle: Alasdair Jardine
240 bottom: Alasdair Jardine
241 top: Alasdair Jardine
242 middle: Fabienne Delafraye
247: Dennis Beauvais
251 top: photos courtesy of Solardome Industries Limited
252 top: Steffen Jaenicke
257 top: Eric Staudenmaier
257 bottom: Miran Kambic
258 top: Michael Jones
260 top: Ph. Giovanni De Sandre
260 middle: Ph. Giovanni De Sandre
261 top: Edmund Sumner
269 top: Gerard van Hees
272 middle: Raffaella Sirtoli
276 top: Jonathan Turner
278 top: Terry Rishel
281 left: Guus Rijven
285 bottom: Anthony Crook
290 middle: Steve Speller
291 middle: David Bird
293: Kenneth Ek
296 top: George Erml
302 bottom: photo by Robaard/Theuwkens, styling by Marjo Kranenborg, CMK
315 top: Ichiro Sugioka
318 middle: Ulla Nyeman
337 top: © Kenkoon
348 bottom: Olympia Sprenger/Hamburg